PUBLISHERS

Employment Law Answer Book
Sixth Edition

by Mark R. Filipp and James Ottavio Castagnera

The last few years have witnessed extraordinary developments in many areas of employment law. United States Supreme Court rulings, legislation, and the increasing globalization of our economy have combined to alter the landscape. *Employment Law Answer Book* provides analysis of the latest judicial and legislative developments in employment law and provides nuts and bolts approaches to legal issues affecting the workplace. It is designed to provide quick, accurate and up-to-date answers to employers, human resources managers, lawyers, and all professionals who need current information about employment law.

Highlights of the 2007 Supplement

This supplement to the Sixth Edition includes analysis of the latest cases, statutes, and developments, including:

- Immigration reform legislation and the direction it is heading in Congress.

- Recent U.S. Supreme Court decisions, including *Smith v. City of Jackson, Mississippi*, which recognized disparate impact as a viable theory of recovery under the Age Discrimination in Employment Act (ADEA), and *IBP v. Alvarez*, which addressed the issue of whether donning and doffing unique safety gear is working time covered by the Fair Labor Standards Act (FLSA).

- Recent cases under the ADEA grappling with the issue of how much disparity in age is sufficient between a former employee and the employee's replacement to maintain an ADEA claim.

- Recent cases under the Americans with Disabilities Act (ADA), including cases analyzing whether "interacting with others" is a major life activity.

- Recent cases involving the application of the Equal Pay Act.

- The evolution of case law determining the application of labor laws to illegal aliens following the U.S. Supreme Court decision in *Hoffman Plastic Compound v. NLRB*, which held that illegal aliens had no redress under the National Labor Relations Act (NLRA).

- Discussion of recent Title VII and Pregnancy Discrimination Act cases.

- Recent cases involving invasion of privacy claims attendant to increased monitoring and surveillance in the workplace.

- Recent cases involving the enforceability of non-competition agreements.

- Practical advice on avoiding employee claims.

- The probability of an avian flu pandemic in the coming months and precautions employers and their employees should be taking.

10/06

For questions concerning this shipment, billing, or other customer service matters, call our Customer Service Department at 1-800-234-1660.

For toll-free ordering, please call 1-800-638-8437.

a Wolters Kluwer business

Employment Law
Answer Book

2007 Supplement

Employment Law Answer Book

Sixth Edition

2007 Supplement

Mark R. Filipp
James Ottavio Castagnera

ΛSPEN

PUBLISHERS

76 Ninth Avenue, New York, NY 10011
www.aspenpublishers.com

This publication is designed to provide accurate and authoritative information in regard to the subject matter covered. It is sold with the understanding that the publisher is not engaged in rendering legal, accounting, or other professional services. If legal advice or other professional assistance is required, the services of a competent professional person should be sought.

—From a *Declaration of Principles* jointly adopted by
a Committee of the American Bar Association and
a Committee of Publishers and Associations

© 2007 Aspen Publishers, Inc.
a Wolters Kluwer business
www.aspenpublishers.com

Printed in the United States of America

ISBN 0-7355-6010-2

1 2 3 4 5 6 7 8 9 0

About Aspen Publishers

Aspen Publishers, headquartered in New York City, is a leading information provider for attorneys, business professionals, and law students. Written by preeminent authorities, our products consist of analytical and practical information covering both U.S. and international topics. We publish in the full range of formats, including updated manuals, books, periodicals, CDs, and online products.

Our proprietary content is complemented by 2,500 legal databases, containing over 11 million documents, available through our Loislaw division. Aspen Publishers also offers a wide range of topical legal and business databases linked to Loislaw's primary material. Our mission is to provide accurate, timely, and authoritative content in easily accessible formats, supported by unmatched customer care.

To order any Aspen Publishers title, go to *www.aspenpublishers.com* or call 1-800-638-8437.

To reinstate your manual update service, call 1-800-638-8437.

For more information on Loislaw products, go to *www.loislaw.com* or call 1-800-364-2512.

For Customer Care issues, e-mail CustomerCare@aspenpublishers.com; call 1-800-234-1660; or fax 1-800-901-9075.

Aspen Publishers
a Wolters Kluwer business

Preface

Since the Fifth Edition was published, we have witnessed major developments in many areas of employment law. Numerous U.S. Supreme Court rulings, legislative enactments, and administrative regulations have combined to alter the landscape—and the liability of employers in the workplace. *Employment Law Answer Book, Sixth Edition*, analyzes these changes with a thorough discussion of the breadth of employment law. This edition provides "nuts and bolts" approaches to responding to the types of issues typically faced by employers. It is designed to provide quick, accurate, and up-to-date answers to employers, human resources managers, lawyers, and all professionals who need current information about employment law.

Some notable areas of discussion and analysis include:

- The growing use of ADR and its implications for employers
- The continuing evolution of Title VII, the ADA, the ADEA, harassment, and retaliation law
- HIPAA privacy rules and other privacy issues
- DOL's new FLSA regulations for exempt employees
- Recent attempts by courts to define and interpret important U.S. Supreme Court decisions, involving such areas as the FMLA and the rights of illegal aliens
- Policies and procedures aimed at reducing risk and exposure to employment claims

With its close scrutiny of judicial, administrative, and legislative changes and detailed coverage of developing issues in employment law, *Employment Law Answer Book, Sixth Edition*, works to ensure that employers and labor law professionals have the latest and most up-to-date information at their fingertips. That knowledge, together with sensible, practical suggestions for putting it to work, will open clearer paths through the ever-growing thicket of employment law.

Employment Law Answer Book, Sixth Edition, provides comprehensive current information on employment law in an easy-to-use question-and-answer format using simple, straightforward language and avoiding technical jargon wherever possible. Numerous examples illustrate how different laws have been applied in specific cases. Citations are provided in brackets as research aids to those who wish to pursue particular subjects in greater detail. For additional assistance in locating related topics, there is an extensive system of cross-referencing to relevant material in other sections of the text.

Format. The question-and-answer format breaks down complex subject areas into concise units. Introductory text provides an overview of the subject that is covered in detail in the questions and answers.

Numbering System. A point system of numbers is used for questions that supplement original material. For example, questions that augment material discussed in Q 1:1 would be numbered Q 1:1.1, Q 1:1.2, and so on. When a question is updated, it is repeated in its entirety.

List of Questions. The detailed list of questions that follows the table of contents helps the reader locate areas of immediate interest. A series of subheadings organizes questions by topic within each chapter.

Tables. To facilitate access to the U.S. Code, Code of Federal Regulations, and cases, tables referenced to question numbers are included.

Index. A detailed topical index is provided as a further aid to locating specific information. All references are to question numbers rather than page numbers.

Use of Abbreviations. Because of the breadth of subject area, a number of terms and statutory references are abbreviated throughout *Employment Law Answer Book*. Among the most common of these shorthand references are:

- Code—The Internal Revenue Code of 1986
- ERISA—The Employee Retirement Income Security Act of 1974, as amended
- EEOC—Equal Employment Opportunity Commission
- IRS—The Internal Revenue Service
- DOL—The U.S. Department of Labor
- COBRA—The Consolidated Omnibus Budget Reconciliation Act of 1985

Mark R. Filipp, J.D.
James Ottavio Castagnera, J.D., Ph.D.
September 2006

About the Authors

Mark R. Filipp is a shareholder and director of Kemp, Klein, Umphrey, Endelman and May, P.C. in Troy, Michigan. He practices almost exclusively in the labor and employment area, primarily representing management. Mr. Filipp has defended a vast array of employment lawsuits, including defense of claims alleging wrongful discharge, discrimination, sexual harassment, retaliatory discharge, and hearings and appeals before various administrative bodies including state agencies and the EEOC. In addition, Mr. Filipp provides regular counsel to employers concerning such matters as reductions in force and employee discipline. Mr. Filipp is a regular speaker on employment law, having conducted numerous seminars and in-house training sessions for employers on such matters as the ADA, FMLA, and sexual harassment. He has authored or co-authored many other publications, including *Covenants Not to Compete, Third Edition* and *The Practical Guide to Employment Law*, both published by Aspen Publishers.

Mr. Filipp received his J.D. from the University of Detroit School of Law in 1981 and was the Editor-in-Chief of the Law Review and recipient of the Clarence M. Burton Scholar award. He received his B.A. degree with honors from Michigan State University. He is active in the State Bar of Michigan, having served as past Chairperson of the Law Practice Management Section and current Member of the Labor and Employment Section. He is also active in the Oakland County Bar Association.

James Ottavio Castagnera, J.D., Ph.D., has spent the past 25 years practicing, writing about, and teaching law. He has been a labor lawyer and litigator with a major Philadelphia firm and the general counsel/corporate secretary for the then-largest convenience store chain in New Jersey and for the nation's number one econometric forecasting organization. In addition to the *Employment Law Answer Book*, he has published 11 other law books and two young-adult novels, as well as some 50 professional/scholarly articles and book chapters. He is a frequent commentator in newspapers, magazines, and broadcast media and writes a regular weekly column called "Attorney at Large." His teaching has taken him to the University of Texas-Austin, the University of Pennsylvania, and the Widener University School of Law. He has just completed his tenth year as Associate Provost and Associate Counsel for

Academic Affairs at Rider University in Princeton/Lawrenceville (NJ), where he also holds the rank of Associate Professor of Business Policy. Mr. Castagnera is also the president of two consulting companies, Pinnacle Employment Law Institute (freelance writing and editing services) and Daybreak Interventions (public relations and conflict/crisis management services).

Acknowledgments

In the *Sixth Edition*, our primary goal was to provide practical and useful information in areas we have found to pose potential difficulty for management. This was a significant undertaking. However, with the invaluable assistance provided by many, including the wonderful editorial guidance from our publisher, we think you will find that our goal has been achieved. In particular, we would like to thank and acknowledge Thomas L. Boyer, J.D., shareholder and director of Kemp, Klein, Umphrey, Endelman and May, P.C., Troy, Michigan, for his many past contributions to this work.

Contents

CHAPTER **5**

Personnel Files and Privacy Issues 5-1

CHAPTER **6**

Security Issues 6-1

CHAPTER **7**

Job Safety 7-1

CHAPTER **13**

CHAPTER **14**

CHAPTER **15**

TABLES

INDEX

List of Questions

Chapter 1 The Legal Framework

Federal Employment Law

Chapter 3 Hiring and Evaluating Employees

Negligent Hiring

Assessing Honesty in Applicants and Employees

Chapter 8 Employee Compensation and Fringe Benefits

Exemptions

Compensation and Withholding

Employee Retirement Income Security Act

The Family and Medical Leave Act

COBRA and HIPAA

Chapter 9 Government Contractors

Security Clearances

Affirmative Action

Wages and Benefits

Chapter 10 Public Employees

Collective Bargaining

Federal Employees

State Employees

Constitutional and Civil Rights

Occupational Health and Safety

Chapter 11 Labor Unions

Bargaining Units and Related Employment Practices

Chapter 12 Immigration and Naturalization

Basics

Discrimination Against Aliens

Immigration Act of 1990

Relationship of Other Laws to Aliens and Immigration

The Immigration Act of 2006

Chapter 13 Employment Termination

Plant Closings, Mass Layoffs, and WARN

Chapter 14 Managing Labor and Employment Litigation

Avoiding Employee Claims

Chapter 15 Employment Law in the Global Marketplace

International Labor Relations

International Organizations

Chapter 1

The Legal Framework

Few areas in the law are as regulated and specialized as employment law. Its legal framework contains a vast array of federal legislation, executive orders, state legislation, and common law—all of which affect the employment relationship from hiring to termination and beyond. Virtually every employment decision that an employer makes has some bearing or relevance to federal or state law. As a result, compliance with regulatory statutes and avoidance of employment litigation is a challenging task. This chapter provides updates on selected recent developments in federal law.

Federal Employment Law

Q 1:25 Have there been any recent developments involving the FMLA?

The regulations implementing the FMLA prepared by the Department of Labor [29 C.F.R. §§ 825.100 *et seq.*] provide that employers who provide leave benefits (paid or unpaid) in addition to the FMLA can designate leaves of absence taken in connection with employer-provided leave benefits as FMLA leave, and it can be counted against FMLA leave time provided the leave qualifies as FMLA leave and the employer promptly notifies the employee of such designation, typically within two business days after acquiring knowledge of its applicability to the FMLA. [29 C.F.R. § 825.208] The regulations specifically provide that if the employer fails to make the appropriate designation, the leave does not count against the employee's FMLA entitlement. [29 C.F.R. § 825.700(a)]

Recently, the penalty for failure to designate leave time as FMLA leave was challenged by an employer who had provided an employee 30 weeks of leave under its own policies. The U.S. Supreme Court, in *Ragsdale v. Wolverine World Wide, Inc.* [535 U.S. 81 (2002)], held that the regulation, which forfeits an employer's right to allocate leave under its own policies to FMLA if it fails to designate the leave was a penalty, went beyond the authority of the Department of Labor.

The *Ragsdale* decision was followed in *Thompson v. Diocese of Saginaw* [2004 WL 45519 (E.D. Mich. Jan. 6, 2004)]. In that case, the employee had been unable to work from August 2000 until March 2001 due to her pregnancy and birth of her child. At no time during her absences was any time off designated by the company as qualifying for FMLA leave, as required by the FMLA regulations. Although the regulations provide that an employer may not designate leave as FMLA leave retroactively, following *Ragsdale*, the court concluded that an employer's violation of the notice regulations does not automatically entitle an employee to additional leave beyond 12 weeks. Rather, an employee must demonstrate that he or she has suffered prejudice by the employer's failure to properly notify him or her of the allocation of the time off to FMLA leave. Recognizing that the plaintiff could not have returned to work within 12 weeks after her leave commenced, regardless of the notice from the company, the court concluded that she could not avail herself of protections under the Act. Simply put, an employee who does not return to work within the 12-week period after a leave commences may not claim protections under the Act.

The *Ragsdale* ruling was also followed by the Third Circuit in *Fogleman v. Greater Hazelton Health Alliance* [2004 WL 2965392 (3d Cir. Dec. 23, 2004)]. In that case, an employee who had not been advised of her FMLA rights had been on a leave that extended beyond 12 weeks. Following *Ragsdale*, the court found that in order to show prejudice, the employee was required to demonstrate that had she been advised of her FMLA rights, she could have returned to work after the 12-week period. However, the testimony in the case indicated that the employee was not able to return to her position at the expiration of the 12-week period, and as such, there was no prejudice for the employer having failed to provide notice to the employee of her FMLA rights.

However, one of the more onerous aspects of the FMLA from management's perspective was upheld by the Sixth Circuit. The FMLA regulations provide that an employee need only provide verbal notice sufficient to make the employer aware that the employee needs time off for an FMLA-qualifying event. [29 C.F.R. § 825.302] The employee need not even mention the FMLA. In *Gerking v. Wabash Ford/Sterling Truck Sales, Inc.* [WL 31045367 (S.D. Ind. Sept. 6, 2002)], the court upheld that verbal notice in and of itself was sufficient. In that case, Gerking had notified his boss of the need for time off for an FMLA-qualifying event but refused to fill out company-required paperwork in connection with the leave (paperwork not required by FMLA regulations). The company attempted to defeat Gerking's reinstatement by maintaining that Gerking was not on FMLA leave because of his failure to execute company-required paperwork. The court held that verbal notice was sufficient under the regulations. [*See* 19 *Employment Discrimination Report (EDR)* (BNA), 371 (Oct. 2, 2002)]

Verbal communication may even be sufficient when the medical condition that requires absences from work is yet to be diagnosed. In *Lincoln v. Sears Home Improvement Products, Inc.* [2004 WL 62716 (D. Minn. Jan. 9, 2004)], an employee communicated to his supervisor a need for time off attributable to his parents' medical conditions. Although the company claimed the details surrounding the medical conditions were "sketchy" and/or "convoluted," the employee had communicated to the company that his father was undergoing surgery, that his mother was ill and depressed, and that he needed to be with them. The company sought to have the FMLA aspects of the case dismissed for lack of proper notification of a need for FMLA leave and the lack of any medical diagnosis as it related to the mother's depressed condition. The court refused to dismiss the FMLA claims, finding that the employee had provided adequate notice of a need for time off attributable to the employee's father and declined to award summary judgment to the company based on the mother's undiagnosed illness.

As to the issue of undiagnosed illnesses, *Helfrich v. Leheigh Valley Hospital* [2003 WL 23162431 (E.D. Pa. Dec. 23, 2003)] is particularly on point. In the case, an employee who was experiencing serious migraine headaches and blurred vision took time off from work to undergo medical evaluations for his condition. Although his condition did not incapacitate him from being able to work, his symptoms resulted in his doctor's request that he undergo further medical evaluations to determine the cause of his symptoms. Although the employee did not allege that he was incapable of performing his job, the court, in reading the FMLA, concluded that a serious health condition under the FMLA also includes situations where employees take time off for purposes of medical evaluation and diagnosis. As the court stated, "It seems unlikely that Congress intended to punish people who are unlucky enough to develop new diseases or suffer serious symptoms for some period of time before the medical profession is able to diagnose the cause of the problem."

In a challenge to the city's policy of denying annual leave bonuses to employees who used sick pay, in *Chubb v. City of Omaha, Nebraska* [424 F.3d 831 (8th Cir. 2005)], the Eighth Circuit held that the policy did not violate the FMLA discrimination provisions as applied to an employee who had taken sick leave during an FMLA leave because the employee elected to use sick pay, something not required under the FMLA.

As to damages under the FMLA, and considering that emotional damages are not contained within the damages expressly provided for under the statute and regulations, the court in *Brumbalough v. Camelot Care Center, Inc.* [427 F.3d 996 (6th Cir. 2005)] held that emotional damages are not recoverable under the FMLA.

Q 1:29 Have there been any recent developments in the area of sexual harassment law?

The area of sexual harassment continues to be subject to constant change and development. Although the EEOC has long maintained that a man as well as a woman may be a victim of sexual harassment and a woman, as well as a man, may be the harasser, so-called same-sex harassment cases have divided many courts. Some courts have maintained that because sexual harassment is a form of gender discrimination, same-sex harassment is not actionable under Title VII. Other courts have argued that there is no logical reason to deny relief to somebody who is harassed by somebody of the same gender, as opposed to someone of the opposite gender. In *Oncale v. Sundowner Offshore Services, Inc.* [535 U.S. 75 (1998)], the U.S. Supreme Court resolved this dispute by allowing claims of same-sex sexual harassment.

The U.S. Supreme Court, in the companion cases of *Burlington Industries, Inc. v. Ellerth* [524 U.S. 775 (1998)] and *Faragher v. City of Boca Raton* [542 U.S. 742 (1998)], provided further guidance on the issue of employer liability for a supervisor's harassment, holding that an employer is vicariously liable for sexual harassment by a supervisor, subject only to an affirmative defense if the employer can demonstrate that the victim failed to take reasonable advantage of the employer's policies and procedures aimed at preventing and correcting harassment, in the instances where no tangible job detriment has been suffered.

In *Cherry v. Bernard Inc.* [No. C99–4029 (N.D. Iowa, Jun. 15, 2000)], a federal district court in Iowa held that a tangible job detriment can be maintained in situations where an employee quits his or her job, but the circumstances are so intolerable as to amount to a constructive discharge. [*See* "Constructive Discharge Is Tangible Action in Sexual Harassment Case, Court Decides," 15 *Employment Discrimination Report (EDR)* (BNA) 76 (Jul. 19, 2000)] In *Suders v. Easton* [325 F.3d 432 (3d Cir. 2003)], the Third Circuit followed *Cherry*, holding that constructive discharge is tantamount to a discharge such that it is to be treated as a tangible adverse employment action.

Since the *Ellerth* and *Faragher* decisions, employers, mindful of the requirements enunciated in these cases, need to undertake efforts to prevent and correct harassment for purposes of maintaining the affirmative defense. Typically, such measures include publication of a sexual harassment policy with a complaint procedure, training supervisors and other employees regarding sexual harassment, encouraging the internal reporting of complaints where harassment is thought to occur, investigating complaints of harassment, and taking appropriate remedial measures. Now, more than ever, employers need to understand the necessity to educate, encourage, and investigate complaints of harassment, lest an employer's failure to take appropriate preventative and corrective action erodes the ability of the employer to take full advantage of the affirmative defense. (See chapter 4 for more recent decisions and other developments.)

In both the *Ellerth* and *Faragher* decisions, the Court reiterated language from earlier decisions that harassment is actionable only if it is so "severe or pervasive" as to "alter the conditions" of the employee's employment and create an "abusive working environment." [*See Faragher*, 524 U.S. at 786, and *Ellerth*, 524 U.S. at 752] In a retaliation case, the U.S. Supreme Court ruled that a single isolated incident wherein a supervisor read aloud a comment made by an applicant in a report, "I hear making love to you is like making love to the Grand Canyon," was such that "no reasonable person could have believed that the single incident recounted above violated Title VII's Standard." [Clark County Sch. Dist. v. Breeden, 532 U.S. 268, 271 (2001)]

Similarly, in *Walpole v. City of Mesa* [162 Fed. Appx. 715 (9th Cir. 2006)], the court held that an employee's romantic interest in a co-employee after a nine-month friendship (culminating in hand holding, professed love, and a request for a kiss which was refused), coupled with staring, was not sufficiently severe or pervasive to amount to sexual harassment.

As to the issue of retaliation, although the court held that a hospital could not avoid liability for the alleged harassment of a nurse because the alleged harasser was a physician independent contractor, the physician's alleged conduct of making nasty and uncivil remarks to the nurse in an attempt to persuade the nurse to drop her complaint of harassment was not an adverse employment action necessary to maintain a retaliation claim against her employer. [Dunn v. Washington County Hosp., 429 F.3d 689 (7th Cir. 2003)]

Q 1:35   How do you determine whether a violation of the Equal Pay Act has occurred?

To determine whether a violation under the Equal Pay Act (EPA) has occurred, a court must analyze the job duties and responsibilities of the positions at issue to determine if they are the same thereby warranting the same pay. In *Brickey v. Employers Reassurance Corp.* [293 F. Supp. 2d 1227 (D. Kan. 2003)], a municipal bond portfolio manager claimed that her employer violated the EPA by paying a male municipal bond portfolio manager substantially more money for substantially equal work. The company claimed that although both the female claimant and her male counterpart were both municipal bond portfolio managers, the male employee had materially different job responsibilities warranting the difference in pay. Specifically, the company claimed that the male employee retained managerial and supervisory responsibilities that his female counterpart did not have, and that the male employee managed larger municipal bond portfolio bond assets and generated greater revenues than his female counterpart. In addition, the company pointed to other factors aside from sex to explain the disparity, including the male portfolio manager's prior salary at a previous company, his reputation, and his experience. Based on these factors, the company moved for summary disposition, but the court, in analyzing both the pay differential and duties and responsibilities of both employees, concluded that there remained genuine issues of fact to be resolved by a jury and denied the company's motion for summary judgment. Specifically, the court noted that, even prior to assuming supervisory responsibilities, the male counterpart received bonuses and compensation well in excess of the female manager, and during testimony, a company manager refused to state that there was any direct correlation between an employee's salary and the value of an employee's portfolio.

A determination of whether the EPA has been violated necessarily requires a comparative analysis of at least two positions in the company. As demonstrated above, position titles are less important than the actual work that the individual and the individual's counterpart actually performed. This point was well made when a female employee sued her prior employer claiming violations of Kentucky's Equal Pay Act, whose language is similar to the federal EPA. Although the female employee claimed that she performed work equal to that of male employees at the office—and was paid substantially less—the court concluded that the position she assumed, environmental specialist, was a new position at the company. No other employee performed the work she did, and as a result, she could not establish a prima facie claim for a violation of the EPA. As the court stated: "Admittedly, the circumstances [no comparables] make allegations of an equal pay violation difficult to sustain." [Wiseman v. Whayne Supply Co., 359 F. Supp. 2d 579 (W.D. Ky. 2004)]

Following the termination of a male bank vice president, a female cashier was promoted to a position of vice president. However, she was not paid as much as the other male vice presidents at the company and filed a claim under the EPA. In comparing her job responsibilities, as opposed to job title, with other vice presidents, the court concluded that although she assumed various duties of the male vice president that she replaced, she did not have the responsibilities of the other vice presidents or her predecessor warranting equal pay. Although she claimed, "If someone is going to be promoted to the title of vice president, they should have sufficient duties and responsibilities to warrant a vice president's pay," the court concluded that job titles and job classifications are not dispositive and ultimately the actual responsibilities and work in the positions will be examined to determine whether there has been a violation of the EPA. Not surprisingly, the court affirmed summary judgment on this issue. [Tenkku v. Normandy Bank, 348 F.3d 737, 741 (8th Cir. 2003)]

The importance of analyzing the actual work and duties performed, as opposed to a position or even written job descriptions was highlighted in *Horn v. University of Minnesota*. [362 F.3d 1042 (8th Cir. 2004)] In that case, the University posted openings for an "Assistant Women's Ice Hockey" position, and two employees were hired for the positions—a man and a woman. The positions had identical job descriptions and titles in their contracts with the University. However, the male coach position paid $2,000 a month while the female coach received $3,000 a month. Despite the identical job descriptions in the posting and contracts, the court analyzed the two positions and concluded that the female assistant coach performed duties significantly in excess of those of the male assistant coach. The female coach, in addition to administrative duties the male coach performed, also performed significant public relations duties for which she had prior skill and experience and which the court concluded prevented the two positions from being "substantially equal" under the EPA.

It is important to note that when wages are compared to determine whether there is in fact a wage disparity under the EPA, courts generally review all forms of remuneration received by the parties for purposes of making the comparison. For example, in the case of *Ghirardo v. University of Southern California* [156 Fed. Appx. 914 (9th Cir. 2005)], the employee claimed that her annual raises were less than those of her male colleagues performing similar work. However, the court concluded that she failed to show that her total compensation was less than the average compensation earned by her male colleagues who performed substantially equal work, and entered summary judgment in favor of the university. [*See also* 29 C.F.R. § 1620.10, which defines *wages* to include "all payments" made to the employee as remuneration for employment, and all forms of compensation.]

Q 1:43.1   How can a claim of discrimination be maintained under the ADA?

A prima facie case of discrimination under the ADA can be maintained if the employee can demonstrate that (1) the employee is disabled within the meaning of the ADA; (2) the employee is qualified and able to perform the essential functions of the job with or without reasonable accommodation; and (3) the employee was terminated or not hired because of the employee's disability. [White v. York Int'l Corp., 45 F.3d 357, 360–61 (10th Cir. 1995)] To be disabled under the ADA, the individual must have a physical or mental impairment that substantially limits one or more major life activity, a record of such an impairment, or been regarded as having such an impairment. [42 U.S.C. § 12102(2)]

Once a prima facie case can be maintained, the burden shifts to the employer to articulate a legitimate nondiscriminatory reason for the adverse employment action at issue. [Castaneda v. East Otero Sch. Dist. R-1, 2005 WL 3280240 (D Colo.)] Once a legitimate nondiscriminatory reason is articulated, it is incumbent upon the plaintiff to demonstrate that the employer's proffered nondiscriminatory reason for the adverse employment action is really a pretext for discrimination. As in *Castaneda*, if the employee is able to raise evidence that casts doubt or raises questions as to the legitimacy or validity of the employer's proffered reasons for the adverse employment action, the case will then typically survive summary disposition and proceed to trial. [*See also* Smith v. District of Columbia, 430 F.3d 450 (D.C. Cir. 2005)]

Q 1:43.2   How do you determine whether somebody is "disabled" under the ADA?

The threshold issue in any ADA case is whether the individual is, has a history of, or is regarded as being disabled. To be disabled, an individual must have, have a history of, or be regarded as having a physical or mental impairment that substantially limits one or more major life activity. [42 U.S.C. § 12102(2)(A)] Even if an individual has a recognized "impairment," if it does not substantially limit one or more major life activity, as defined under the regulations, it will not be sufficient to qualify as a disability under the ADA. For example, recognized major life activities include walking, hearing, seeing, breathing, working, and the like. [*See* Chenoweth v. Hillsborough, CY, 250 F.3d 1328, 1329 (11th Cir. 2001)] In *Reberg v. Road Equipment* [2005 WL 3320780 (N.D. Ind.)], a recognized impairment, a sleep disorder, was held not to be a substantial limitation of a major life activity when it prevented the employee truck driver only from driving long distances. Likewise, a bipolar disorder that was found to be a mental impairment was nonetheless found not to limit the employee substantially in one or more life activity, even though the employee had difficulty interacting with others and working on occasion. [*See* Price v. Facilities Mgmt. Group, Inc., 403 F. Supp. 2d 1246 (N.D. Ga. 2005)]

Q 1:45 Have there been any recent developments regarding the ADA?

Although unchanged from its initial wording, the ADA continues to evolve with respect to its interpretation and applicability. A growing trend, which began as early as 1993, was for federal courts to apply a so-called "medicated" standard to determine whether a person is a qualified individual with a disability, entitled to protection against discrimination under the ADA. By using a medicated, as opposed to non-medicated, standard, an individual with a medical condition who with medication can substantially perform major life functions is not protected from discrimination under the ADA. In recent years, a growing number of courts appeared to be accepting the medicated standard approach. In the long-awaited companion decisions of *Sutton v. United Air Lines, Inc.* [527 U.S. 471 (1999)] and *Murphy v. United Parcel Services, Inc.* [527 U.S. 516 (1999)], the Supreme Court held that mitigating measures an employee takes, both positive and negative (such as drug therapy and other corrective measures), must be taken into consideration when analyzing whether an individual is disabled (whether the mental or physical impairment substantially limits a major life activity), and therefore entitled to protection under the ADA.

The Supreme Court also reaffirmed the EEOC's long-stated position that individuals who are not actually disabled may nonetheless be protected by the ADA if an employer takes action against an employee or applicant based on the mistaken notion that an employee is disabled, even if he or she actually is not. Under *Sutton*, an individual is "regarded as" disabled if the employer mistakenly believes the employee has an impairment that substantially limits one or more major life activities. As to limitations involving the ability to perform a job, the mistaken perception of a restriction must apply to a class of jobs or broad range of jobs within a class, not just one particular job or specialized position. In January 2001, a federal court in Minnesota, citing *Sutton*, permitted a "regarded as" claim instituted by the EEOC to go to trial against a company that allegedly discriminated against an employee because of a mistaken perception of a disability after the employee suffered a heart attack. [16 *Employment Discrimination Report (EDR)* (BNA) 342 (Mar. 7, 2001)]

Another issue is whether an individual self-certified as "totally disabled" for Social Security purposes can still maintain an ADA claim, which requires that the individual be able to perform the essential functions of a job, with or without accommodation. This apparent contradiction in position had split the circuits, and in *Cleveland v. Policy Management Systems Corp.* [526 U.S. 795 (1999)], the Supreme Court ruled that self-certification of "total disability" for purposes of obtaining Social Security benefits was not a per se bar to the ability of an employee to file an ADA claim. The Court noted that to maintain the claim the employee would have to proffer sufficient explanation for the apparent contradiction.

In March 1999, the EEOC issued its long-awaited "Policy Guidance on Reasonable Accommodation under the ADA" [12 *Employment Discrimination Report (EDR)* (BNA) 317 (Mar. 3, 1999)], providing further instructions on the measures companies must consider when analyzing and implementing accommodations for qualified persons with disabilities.

With respect to emerging issues involving genetic testing, in March 2000 EEOC Commissioner Paul Miller reiterated the EEOC's long-held position that discrimination based on genetic testing violates the "regarded as" prong under the ADA. [14 *Employment Discrimination Report (EDR)* (BNA) 432 (Mar. 29, 2000)] The Burlington Northern Santa Fe Railroad stated that it would stop the practice of genetically testing workers with carpal tunnel syndrome after the EEOC instituted litigation against the Railroad for violating the ADA. [16 *Employment Discrimination Report (EDR)* (BNA) 221 (Feb. 14, 2001)]

In *Board of Trustees of the University of Alabama v. Garrett* [531 U.S. 356 (2001)], the Court held that the ADA does not apply to states, finding that it was not Congress' intent to abrogate the States' Eleventh Amendment immunity when enacting the ADA. In *Toyota Motor Manufacturing Kentucky, Inc. v. Williams* [534 U.S. 184 (2002)], the Court held that for a carpal tunnel syndrome condition alleged to substantially impair the performance of manual tasks, to "substantially impair a major life activity" (a requirement of the ADA), the condition must prevent or restrict the individual from performing activities that are of central importance to most people's daily lives, not just impair the individual's ability to perform the manual tasks of his or her job only. In *US Airways, Inc. v. Barnett* [535 U.S. 391 (2002)], the Court held that a requested accommodation of a union worker that conflicts with seniority rules under a collective bargaining agreement (CBA) is ordinarily sufficient to show that the requested accommodation is unreasonable, absent special circumstances.

The U.S. Supreme Court has issued significant decisions involving the ADA. In *Chevron USA v. Echazabal* [536 U.S. 73 (2002)], the Court settled a dispute among various district courts as to whether an individual's posing a "direct threat" to himself, in connection with performing a job, is a defense to an ADA claim. Although it is well settled that posing a direct threat to others is a defense, courts were split as to whether this defense also included the so-called "threat-to-self" situation. In that case, the employee had a liver condition that would be aggravated by continued exposure to toxins at the employer's refinery, according to the company doctors. Although the statute contains an explicit provision for defense based on threat to others, the EEOC in its regulations has long provided that threat-to-self was also a legitimate defense to an ADA claim, and the Supreme Court agreed.

Although initially established as part of sexual harassment doctrine, a claim of hostile work environment under the ADA has been recognized by many federal circuits. To establish a prima facie claim, the employee must demonstrate that (1) he is a qualified individual with a disability; (2) he was subjected to unwelcome harassment; (3) the harassment was based on his disability; (4) the harassment was sufficiently severe or pervasive to alter a term, condition, or privilege of his employment; and (5) some factual basis exists to impute liability for the harassment to the employer. [*See* Rohan v. Networks Presentations, LLC, 375 F.3d 266 (4th Cir. 2004)]

The determination of whether or not the situation is sufficiently hostile to maintain a claim is viewed under both an objective and subjective analysis, similar to the analysis in sexual harassment cases. In *Edmunson v. Potter* [2004 118 Fed. Appx. 726 (4th Cir. 2004)], an employee with carpal tunnel syndrome claimed that she was subjected to a hostile work environment on account of her disability. In reviewing the alleged acts in support of her claim of hostile work environment, the court concluded that the acts were isolated and ordinary adversities in the workplace, and not sufficiently severe or pervasive when viewed objectively. Recently, the Tenth Circuit joined other circuits that have recognized hostile work environment claims under the ADA. [*See* Lanman v. Johnson County, Kan., 393 F.3d 1151 (10th Cir. 2004)]

One issue that courts have been struggling with is whether "interacting with others" is a major life activity under the ADA. In *Doebele v. Sprint Corp.* [168 F. Supp. 2d 1247, 1261 (D. Kan. 2001)], the Tenth Circuit noted that it had not yet held "interacting with others" to be a major life activity. This issue was recently addressed by the court in *Price v. Facility Management Group, Inc.* [403 F. Supp. 2d 1246 (N.D. Ga. 2005)] In *Price* the employee suffered from bipolar disorder, a clear mental impairment, and claimed that his condition substantially limited his ability to interact with others, which he claimed was a major life activity under the ADA. Recognizing that the Eleventh Circuit has yet to decide whether "interacting with others" is a major life activity, the court held that even assuming that it is a major life activity, the employee had not demonstrated that it is an activity in which he is substantially limited. The plaintiff pointed to his difficulties in dealing with others and various outbursts to maintain the claim, but the court held that the record indicated that he was not "unable" to interact with others—he just occasionally did so in an inappropriate manner. As such, and without having to decide whether "interacting with others" is a major life activity, the court held that the employee's claim failed in this regard.

Q 1:50 Have there been any recent developments regarding the NLRA?

Yes. The U.S. Supreme Court, in *NLRB v. Kentucky River Community Care, Inc.* [582 U.S. 706 (2001)], decided that registered nurses at a mental health facility were "supervisors," such that they were not subject to representation under the NLRA. In a controversial decision, the Supreme Court held that illegal aliens had no right to obtain redress under the NLRA due to their illegal status. [Hoffman Plastic Compounds, Inc. v. NLRB, 535 U.S. 137 (2002)]

Q 1:56 Have there been any recent developments under the IRCA?

Yes. In a somewhat controversial 5–4 decision, the U.S. Supreme Court, in *Hoffman Plastic Compounds, Inc. v. NLRB* [535 U.S. 137 (2002)], held that an illegal alien who utilized false documentation in connection with the I-9 process under IRCA to secure employment could not be provided relief under the NLRA for being fired for union activities—a clear unfair labor practice under the Act.

However, post-*Hoffman* decisions indicate its limitations with many courts as it applies to the rights of illegal aliens working in this country. For example, in the decision in *Madeira v. Affordable Housing Foundation, Inc.* [315 F. Supp. 2d 504 (2004)], the court, although recognizing the *Hoffman* decision, held that it had no applicability to claims under state labor laws. Specifically, the court held that the employee's alien status did not prevent him from recovering compensatory damages for the company's violation of New York labor law. As the court stated:

> And the fact is, undocumented aliens do obtain work in the United States. Recognizing this incontrovertible fact, New York's public does not bar compensation in the form of back pay for undocumented workers who are injured in the manner of the instant plaintiff. [315 F. Supp. 2d at 507]

Not to be outdone, the Ninth Circuit went even further in what may appear to some to be a clear attempt to avoid the apparent mandate of *Hoffman*. In *Rivera v. Nibco, Inc.* [364 F.3d 1057 (9th Cir. 2004)], a number of female immigrants formerly employed by a factory brought an action against their employer alleging national origin discrimination in violation of Title VII. During discovery, the defendant corporation sought to determine the plaintiffs' immigration status, undoubtedly seeking to determine whether they would have a *Hoffman*-based defense to the claims. The plaintiffs refused to provide information regarding their immigration status, and the trial court entered a protective order precluding the employer from using discovery to inquire into the plaintiffs' immigration status. On appeal, the Ninth Circuit concluded that the harm caused by forcing the plaintiffs to disclose their immigration status outweighed any right of the employer to obtain this discovery in that, by revealing their immigration status, any plaintiffs found to be undocumented might face criminal prosecution or deportation. As to *Hoffman*, the court read the decision narrowly and seriously questioned whether it had any applicability to Title VII cases, and concluded it clearly did not speak as to discovery issues. In *Zavala v. Wal-Mart Stores, Inc.* [393 F. Supp. 295 (D. Ct. N.J. 2005)], the court held, in accordance with a growing number of courts, that despite *Hoffman*, illegal aliens still have rights to be paid in accordance with the FLSA for work performed.

Chapter 3

Hiring and Evaluating Employees

This chapter describes the legal aspects of the application process and the evaluation of employee performance. It discusses job advertising, information that can be gathered from the application or interview process, methods of evaluating employee performance, work rules, and employee discipline. Just as chapter 1 demonstrated how federal and state laws have diminished the historic freedom of employers, similarly, these various laws specifically restrain what employers can and cannot do and say in hiring and evaluating the performance of their employees.

Negligent Hiring

Q 3:41   How do courts determine whether an employer has acted negligently in retaining an employee?

The issue of whether or not negligent retention can be maintained depends upon the facts of each case. In *Mils v. Deehr* [2004 WL 1047720 (Ohio App. May 6, 2004)], a parishioner claimed that a church employee had molested and sexually assaulted him and that the church and church management were liable under the doctrine of negligent retention. Although the case was dismissed by the trial court, on appeal the court pointed to allegations involving the church employee's close contact with the parishioner at odd hours on multiple occasions that should have alerted church officials of alleged criminal, tortious, or dangerous conduct. Based on these facts, the court concluded that there were sufficient alleged facts to withstand a motion to dismiss and remanded the matter to the trial court for further proceedings.

In *McClements v. Ford Motor Company* [2004 WL 868255 (Mich. App. Apr. 22, 2004)], an unpublished decision, the plaintiff, an employee for an independent food service company, claimed that Ford Motor Company was negligent in retaining a superintendent who allegedly sexually assaulted her. Although the case was dismissed by the trial court, on appeal the court pointed to numerous prior allegations of sexual harassment regarding the superintendent, as well as a prior conviction of indecent exposure, that should have alerted Ford Motor Company to the superintendent's dangerous propensities. Due to these facts, the court concluded that there were sufficient allegations to allege that Ford Motor Company knew or should have known of the superintendent's propensities such that it could be liable for negligent retention.

However, to state a claim for negligent retention, the allegations of harm must be proximately caused by the negligent retention. In *Spencer, et al. v. Health Force, Inc.* [135 N.M. 554 (N.M. App. 2004)], an employee hired by caregiver Health Force was alleged to have caused the death of the plaintiff's decedent by injecting her with heroin. Apparently, prior to the alleged incident involving the death, there was evidence that the caregiver may have taken the decedent's narcotic prescription pills while on duty. Noting that the negligent retention must be the proximate cause of the plaintiff's injury and injury must be foreseeable, the court concluded that a jury could not reasonably find that the defendant's retention of the caregiver after he allegedly stole three narcotic pills could be considered the proximate cause of the decedent's death more than three weeks later. However, to establish negligent retention, a single prior isolated instance of misconduct may be insufficient to maintain a negligent retention claim.

The issue of whether one single prior incident of misconduct is sufficient for purposes of maintaining a negligent retention claim based on additional misconduct was addressed by the court in *Doe v. ATC, Inc.* [624 S.E.2d 447 (S.C. App. 2005)] In that case, the mother of a disabled adult brought an action against a transportation company based on the bus driver's having allegedly touched her disabled adult daughter inappropriately while she was being "transported" to physical therapy sessions. Several months prior to this bus incident, the bus driver had allegedly made inappropriate sexual advances toward a co-employee, and the incident was reported to a supervisor. The trial court directed a verdict in favor of the transportation company, and, on appeal, the court considered whether, as a matter of law, a single prior incident of misconduct was sufficient for purposes of maintaining a negligent retention case. Although allowing that other states had found that negligent retention requires that the plaintiff demonstrate some propensity, proclivity, or course of conduct sufficient to put the employer on notice of possible dangers to third parties such that a single prior incident of misconduct fails to state a claim for negligent retention as a matter of law, the court held that a single incident of prior misconduct may support a negligent retention claim, provided the prior misconduct has a sufficient nexus to the ultimate harm. However, in this case, the court concluded that the misconduct directed to the co-employee lacked sufficient nexus to the conduct involving the disabled rider and affirmed the dismissal of the case. The court seemed to suggest that had there been a similar prior act of misconduct by the bus driver involving bus riders, it may have held otherwise.

Assessing Honesty in Applicants and Employees

Q 3:45.1   Can a contractor of the government use the national security exemption under the EPPA?

In *Polkey v. Transtecs Corp.* [404 F.3d 1264 (11th Cir. 2005)], a contractor of the Department of Defense (DOD) whose employees must meet a "secret clearance level" from the government, maintained that it was exempted from the EPPA under the national security exception in connection with its administration of a polygraph examination to employees as a result of a "mailroom incident" violating federal law. The court, in reviewing the statute and regulations, held that the national security exemption exists to allow the federal government to take lie detector tests of employees of a contractor of the DOD, but does not allow contractors to conduct the test themselves. As the court held, the national defense exemption applies to the federal government only, and a private contractor's attempt to rely on the national security exemption is misplaced. [*Polkey*, at 1269]

Q 3:45.2   What is the investigation exception under the EPPA?

Under the EPPA, employers investigating theft or other similar occurrences may request that an employee submit to a lie detector test provided that the tested employee had access to the subject of the investigation and the employer had reasonable suspicion that the employee was involved. In *Polkey v. Transtecs Corp.* [404 F.3d 1264 (11th Cir. 2005)], a contractor for the federal government claimed among other things that its administration of lie detector tests fit within the exemption of an ongoing investigation, in that it had reasonable suspicion for the individuals who were asked to take polygraphs and could demonstrate that the employees had access to the subject of the investigation. The case centered around a "mailroom incident," where an employee discovered someone, in violation of federal law, had accessed mail that the contractor was processing. The employer requested a number of employees who had access to the mail to submit to polygraph examinations, which they refused. The employer argued that these employees fell within the investigation exception based on reasonable suspicion and access to the subject matter of the investigation. However, the court concluded that the employer provided no basis for reasonable suspicion. The court held that to maintain a "reasonable suspicion," it must be based upon an "observable articulable basis in fact which indicates that a particular employee was involved and responsible for an economic loss," citing 29 C.F.R. § 801.12(f)(1). [*Polkey*, at 1270] The employer provided no basis for reasonable suspicion other than access to the mail that was the subject of the mailroom incident, and the court concluded that fact, standing alone, did not constitute reasonable suspicion.

Disciplinary Programs and Procedures

Q 3:97 Can an employer be held liable for defamation in connection with employee reviews and/or discipline?

Under common law, to claim actionable defamation, the employee must prove that the alleged defamatory statement was untrue, that it was published to a third party, and that the employer acted with malice. Malice is necessary to overcome the qualified privilege that employers possess in the employment context under common law. In *Lecours v. Mobile Corp.* [2005 WL 3500802 (N.J. Super. A.D. unpublished opinion)], an employee brought a defamation action against his employer based on statements made by his supervisor in e-mail messages about the plaintiff's work performance. In reviewing the e-mail messages, the court concluded that they were "opinions" as opposed to "facts" and that they were similar to employee evaluations, which do not historically qualify as defamation. Moreover, the court concluded, even if the statements were statements of fact, such statements are subject to a qualified privilege in the employment context that can be overcome only if the employee establishes that the publisher knew the statement to be false or acted in reckless disregard of its truth or falsity. With no such evidence in this case, the court confirmed dismissal of the defamation count.

Even if an employee can maintain that the reasons provided in a termination report distributed to employees is false, if the distribution of the report was only to those employees whose duties include handling such reports, there is no "publication," and the defamation claim cannot be maintained at all. In *Smith v. Boyd Bros. Transportation, Inc.* [406 F. Supp. 2d 1238 (M.D. Ala. 2005)], a terminated employee claimed that the statements concerning the reasons for his termination were false and sued the company for publication of the material within the company. The company countered by, among other things, demonstrating that the only people who had access to the report were those whose duties included handling such reports. Citing previous precedent, the court found that this type of internal distribution is insufficient to meet the "publication" requirement for defamation as a matter of law, and dismissed the claim.

However, the qualified privilege has its limitations, as was demonstrated in *Rachal v. State of Louisiana Department of Wildlife & Fisheries.* [918 So.2d 570 (La. App. 3d Cir. 2005)] In that case, employees sued for defamation arising out of a report prepared and disseminated by a supervisor that outlined the details of an alleged telephone call the supervisor received in which the caller reported that he observed the plaintiff employees engaging in sex during working hours. On appeal, the court concluded that, based on the inconsistent testimony of the supervisor and the testimony of the witnesses for the employees, it was questionable whether the supervisor did in fact receive the so-called anonymous call regarding the plaintiffs, but that even if he did receive the anonymous call, it was not error for the jury to conclude that it was not reasonable for the supervisor to believe that it was true. As such, the qualified privilege was overcome in this instance.

Chapter 4

Employment Discrimination

Discrimination law is among the most dynamic areas of labor and employment law in the United States. Since this book was first published in 1988, substantive changes in the statutory law as well as developments in the federal common (court-made) law of employment discrimination have been dramatic. For example, the Americans with Disabilities Act of 1990 (ADA), signed into law by President George Bush, significantly changed how employees with disabilities may be treated in the workplace and whether disability-related inquiries can be made in the application process. During the past five years, sexual harassment law has grown significantly both in its definition of sexual harassment and in how the employer should respond to internal claims of sexual harassment. The area of affirmative action has also changed dramatically in the past few years, shedding what was considered by many to be blind allegiance to antiquated affirmative action and set-aside programs. This chapter updates federal discrimination law by discussing recent developments in this constantly evolving area.

Title VII

Enforcement of Title VII by the EEOC

Q 4:13   How does the EEOC process charges of discrimination?

In late April 1995, the Charge Processing Task Force, under the direction of Vice Chairman Paul Igasaki, made its recommendations for wide-ranging changes in the way charges are processed.

First among the changes is that all new charges must be triaged to one of three categories. Category A charges have high priority because they involve patterns of discrimination and high-profile targets, and their probable cause is likely. Category B charges have merit but require additional investigation. Category C charges are susceptible to dismissal by the EEOC. Before these reforms took effect, EEOC investigators had to work their dockets on a first-come, first-served basis and investigate each charge fully. These reforms allow them to dismiss charges that do not warrant complete investigations and to concentrate their efforts in accordance with the EEOC's National Enforcement Plan, discussed later.

Second, the task force recommendations emphasized settling discrimination claims. Taking its lead from Congress, which in the 1991 Civil Rights Act encourages the use of alternative dispute resolution (ADR) techniques, the EEOC indicated that it will use mediation to settle claims through a nonbinding mediation process using volunteer employment law mediators—a program currently underway.

Third, the EEOC announced its intent to allow its attorneys in its 10 regional offices to exercise increased discretion in deciding which cases to take into federal court. This change will free commissioners to deal with broad policy issues.

The National Enforcement Plan (NEP), developed in 1995, attempts to focus the EEOC's resources on large-scale and egregious cases of employment discrimination. *EEOC v. Mitsubishi Motor Manufacturing of America, Inc.* [No. 96-CV-1192 (D.C. Ill. 1996)] is a good example of a high-profile, allegedly egregious case of sex discrimination that is consistent with the plan.

The triage system, together with efforts to mediate disputes, was instituted for several reasons. One reason was to dispose of those cases that do not merit the use of scarce resources to investigate. The second reason was to focus the EEOC's energies in accordance with its NEP, in order to pursue more serious and significant charges of discrimination. Recent information indicates that, statistically, the 1995 recommendations may have obtained some measure of result. According to information supplied by the EEOC in Spring 1998, and despite the fact that the number of charges nationwide continued to increase from approximately 78,000 in Fiscal Year 1996 to approximately 81,000 in Fiscal Year 1997, the EEOC's backlog of pending matters continued to drop during Fiscal Year 1997 and litigation activity and money recovered for claimants increased during Fiscal Year 1997. [*See* "Commission Reaped Record Benefits, Culled Backlog of Charges Last Year," 10 *Employment Discrimination Report (EDR)* (BNA) 372 (Mar. 25, 1998)] For Fiscal Year 1998, the EEOC reported its backlog of charges continued to decrease, from 65,000 in Fiscal Year 1997 to 52,000 by the end of Fiscal Year 1998, with new charges decreasing slightly from Fiscal Year 1997 (81,000) to Fiscal Year 1998 (79,000). [12 *Employment Discrimination Report (EDR)* (BNA) 183 (Feb. 10, 1999)] For Fiscal Year 1999, the EEOC reported its backlog of unresolved charges to be approximately 40,000, a significant decrease with new charges decreasing slightly to 77,444. [14 *Employment Discrimination Report (EDR)* (BNA) 153 (Feb. 2, 2000)] For Fiscal Year 2000, the EEOC reported its backlog of unresolved charges to be reduced to about 34,300, a record low, with the new charges increasing slightly to 79,900. [16 *Employment Discrimination Report (EDR)* (BNA) 75 (Jan. 17, 2001)] It was reported that Fiscal Year 2001 showed a modest decrease of unresolved charges (32,500), with a slight increase of new charges during the year (80,000). [18 *Employment Discrimination Report (EDR)* (BNA) 259 (Feb. 27, 2002)] Fiscal Year 2002 closed with a pending inventory of just less than 30,000 charges, with an overall increase of total charges filed (84,442). [20 *Employment Discrimination Report (EDR)* (BNA) 106 (Jan. 15, 2003)] In Fiscal Year 2005, the EEOC received 75,428 total charges, less than the 79,432 received in Fiscal Year 2004, and resolved 77,352 charges, leaving the EEOC with a pending inventory of 33,562 in Fiscal Year 2005, a slight increase from 29,966 for Fiscal Year 2004.

No doubt, because of the results of the 1995 recommendations by the Task Force, the EEOC has implemented charge-processing and litigation recommendations. One such recommendation directed the Office of General Counsel and the Office of Field Programs in conjunction with the district offices to develop local enforcement plans (LEP) in order to establish goals unique to the particular community that the district office serves, and that are consistent and developed in accordance with the NEP. The development of the LEP in conjunction with the NEP signals the EEOC's continuing effort to focus its energies on those issues of discrimination it deems particularly significant to this society.

Q 4:14 How does the EEOC alternative dispute resolution (ADR) mediation program work?

Another growing development in how the EEOC processes charges is the use of ADR mediation programs to attempt to facilitate and mediate charges after they are filed. Although conciliation has always been part of the investigative process, the EEOC has not traditionally processed claims by using a separate ADR process. The ADR project, which started in 1993–1994 as a pilot voluntary project in Washington, D.C., Houston, New Orleans, and Philadelphia, was expanded to various districts throughout the country. In October 1998, Congress designated $13 million of the EEOC's budget for further expansion of ADR. Currently, the EEOC Mediation Program is being implemented nationwide, as an alternative to the traditional investigative process.

In accordance with the program, local district EEOC offices review charges of discrimination and determine whether they would be suitable for ADR. If so, the district office invites the parties to participate in a voluntary nonbinding ADR process, used to assist in voluntary settlement of the EEOC charges. Either party can deny the invitation, without recourse, at which point the matter is forwarded to the assigned investigator for traditional charge processing, including investigation. If both parties agree to take advantage of the ADR program, the parties are assigned a federal mediator—an outside individual who is not involved in the investigation of the charge for the EEOC—who will meet with the parties and attempt to assist them in determining whether there is any mutually agreeable basis for resolution of the charge. The information discussed during the mediation is confidential and not shared with the EEOC investigator, should the matter not be resolved. The program appears to be successful in relieving the EEOC of the responsibility of investigating charges that can be resolved early on in the proceedings, and the use of ADR in connection with EEOC charges can be expected to become more prevalent in years to come. ADR is clearly viewed by many as an attractive supplement to the traditional administrative and judicial process. [See published text of the EEOC's Mediation Program Fact Sheet, 12 *Employment Discrimination Report (EDR)* (BNA) 244 (Feb. 17, 1999)] Despite the budgetary pressures, the EEOC gave the mediation program high marks for Fiscal Year 2000, claiming to have mediated about 8,000 cases during the year. [See 16 *Employment Discrimination Report (EDR)* (BNA) 76 (Jan. 17, 2001)] Similarly, in Fiscal Year 2001, despite continuing budgetary pressures, Cari Dominguez, chair of the EEOC, stated that more than 7,000 charges were resolved through the mediation program. [See 17 *Employment Discrimination Report (EDR)* (BNA) 641 (Dec. 15, 2001)] In Fiscal Year 2002, the EEOC reportedly resolved almost 8,000 charges through mediation. Dominguez proclaimed that "Mediation will continue to be on center stage during 2003." [20 *Employment Discrimination Report (EDR)* (BNA) 75 (Jan. 15, 2003)] In Fiscal Year 2003, according to the EEOC's website (www.eeoc.gov), the EEOC resolved approximately 70 percent of charges that went through the mediation process, resolving 7,990 charges in total.

The EEOC has posted a number of materials regarding mediation on its website, including a description of the process, common questions and answers, the EEOC's ADR Policy Statement, and a detailed history of the mediation program. [See www.eeoc.gov/mediate.]

National Origin Discrimination

Q 4:45　Do illegal aliens enjoy the same benefits under U.S. labor laws as documented aliens who are authorized to work in the United States?

In a controversial decision, the U.S. Supreme Court ruled that the NLRB could not order a company to give back pay to an illegal alien as a penalty for committing an unfair labor practice (discharging the illegal alien for union activities in violation of the NLRA). [Hoffman Plastic Compounds, Inc. v. NLRB, 535 U.S. 137 (2002)] However, post-*Hoffman* decisions indicate its limitations with many courts as it applies to the rights of illegal aliens working in this country. For example, in the decision in *Madeira v. Affordable Housing Foundation, Inc.* [315 F. Supp. 2d 504 (2004)], the court, although recognizing the *Hoffman* decision, held that it had no applicability to claims under state labor laws. Specifically, the court held that the employee's alien status as an illegal alien did not prevent him from recovering compensatory damages for the company's violation of New York labor law. As the court stated:

> And the fact is, undocumented aliens do obtain work in the United States. Recognizing this incontrovertible fact, New York's public does not bar compensation in the form of back pay for undocumented workers who are injured in the manner of the instant plaintiff. [315 F. Supp. 2d 504, 507]

Not to be outdone, the Ninth Circuit went even further in what may appear to some to be a clear attempt to avoid the apparent mandate of *Hoffman*. In *Rivera v. Nibco, Inc.*, 364 F. 3d 1057 (9th Cir. 2004), a number of female immigrants formerly employed by a factory brought an action against their employer alleging national origin discrimination in violation of Title VII. During discovery, the defendant corporation sought to determine the plaintiffs' immigration status, undoubtedly seeking to determine whether they would have a *Hoffman*-based defense to the claims. The plaintiffs refused to provide information regarding their immigration status, and the trial court entered a protective order precluding the employer from using discovery to inquire into the plaintiffs' immigration status. On appeal, the Ninth Circuit concluded that the harm caused by forcing the plaintiffs to disclose their immigration status outweighed any right of the employer to obtain this discovery in that, by revealing their immigration status, any plaintiffs found to be undocumented might face criminal prosecution or deportation. As to *Hoffman*, the court read the decision narrowly and seriously questioned whether it had any applicability to Title VII cases, and concluded it clearly did not speak as to discovery issues. In *Zavala v. Wal-Mart Stores, Inc.* [393 F. Supp. 295 (D. Ct. N.J. 2005)], the court joined a growing number of courts and held that illegal aliens are covered by the FLSA.

Discrimination Based on Religion

Q 4:50   What religious practices or beliefs are subject to protection under Title VII?

The EEOC interprets religious practices broadly to include "moral or ethical beliefs as to what is right or wrong, which are sincerely held with the strength of traditional religious views." [29 C.F.R. § 1605.1] Although traditional organized religion certainly falls within the standard for protection under Title VII, sincere beliefs that are not attached to traditional beliefs are also likely afforded protection under Title VII. The EEOC's standard for determining protected religious beliefs is taken from cases defining the scope of conscientious-objector status in the military. [Welsh v. United States, 398 U.S. 333 (1970); United States v. Seeger, 380 U.S. 163 (1965)]

In *Seeger* and *Welsh*, the court was asked to determine whether an individual not affiliated with any traditional denomination can claim conscientious-objector status in the military. Although both Seeger and Welsh claimed to have been brought up in religious environments and to have attended church in their childhoods, neither continued their ties with their native churches into adulthood and neither belonged to or was affiliated with any religious group or adhered to any teaching of an organized religious group as adults. In addition, the organized religion that they observed as children did not teach their members not to engage in war at any time for any reason. Nonetheless, both insisted that they held deep conscientious beliefs against taking part in a war in which people were killed, and both believed that killing in war was wrong, unethical, and immoral. Seeger did not attach any specific belief in relation to any supreme being, but nevertheless decried the "spiritual price" man must pay to engage in killing people in war. Likewise, Welsh neither affirmed nor denied his belief in a supreme being, but left the question open.

Although neither plaintiff ascribed his conscientious-objector status to any organized or traditional religion or belief in a supreme being, the court was satisfied that their beliefs were entitled to as much protection as those derived from traditional religious convictions. As the court stated in *Welsh*:

> Because his beliefs function as a religion in his life, such an individual is as much entitled to a religious conscientious objector exemption under 6(j) as is someone who derives his conscientious objection to war from traditional religious convictions. [398 U.S. 33 at 335]

Following *Welsh* and *Seeger*, the EEOC accords religious protection to sincerely held views of right and wrong that fall outside traditional religious teachings and practices.

Dress and personal grooming habits related to religious beliefs may be subject to protection under religious discrimination law as well. For example, an arbitrator had held that a company did not have good cause to terminate a Muslim employee who refused for religious reasons to tuck in his shirt in accordance with a company dress code policy. [*See* 10 *Employment Discrimination Report (EDR)* (BNA) 42 (Jan. 14, 1998)] Similarly, a U.S. District Court granted an injunction against the suspension of a police officer who refused to cut his dreadlocks, claiming that his dreadlocks were based upon religious beliefs and his African-American culture. [*See* Robinson v. District of Columbia Government, D.C. No. 97–787 (Jul. 17, 1997); 9 *Employment Discrimination Report (EDR)* (BNA) 150] The Fourth Circuit reinstated a correctional officer's claims of religious discrimination based on discipline he received for dreadlocks that he wore based on his Rastafarian religious beliefs. [*See* Booth v. Maryland, No. 02–1657 (4th Cir. Apr. 30, 2003), discussed in 20 *Employment Discrimination Report (EDR)* (BNA) 646 (May 14, 2003)] In *Fraternal Order of Police Newark Lodge No. 12 v. Newark* [3d Cir. No. 97–5342 (Mar. 3, 1999)], the U.S. Court of

Appeals for the Third Circuit held that a no-beard policy, subject only to exceptions for medical reasons, unlawfully discriminated against Muslim officers who grew beards for religious reasons. [*See* 12 *Employment Discrimination Report (EDR)* (BNA) 390 (Mar. 17, 1999)] As a result of a lawsuit instituted by the EEOC [EEOC v. Federal Express Corp., S.D. Ga. No. CV 100–50, consent decree filed May 24, 2001], Federal Express is reported to have agreed to modify its "no beard" policy by permitting employees who wear beards for religious reasons to seek an exception to the policy. [*See* 16 *Employment Discrimination Report (EDR)* (BNA) 868 (Jun. 29, 2001)]

Although it seems that courts are deferential to professed religious beliefs when analyzing claims of religious discrimination, there are limits. For example, in *EEOC v. Allendale Nursing Home Center* [W.D. Mich. No. 1:97-CV-64 (Mar. 6, 1998)], the employee was fired for refusing to provide a Social Security number, claiming that the Social Security Administration was "unbiblical" and that her deeply held religious beliefs did not allow her to obtain a Social Security number. Despite her claim, the court ultimately concluded that the employee's discharge as a result of her refusal to provide a Social Security number was not religious discrimination under Title VII. The Seventh Circuit rejected a similar claim by an applicant who claimed that the Social Security number was the "mark of the beast" and refused to provide it to the employer. The court reasoned that it was not necessary for an employer to violate the Internal Revenue Code in order to accommodate the applicant's professed religious beliefs. [14 *Employment Discrimination Report (EDR)* (BNA) 321 (Mar. 8, 2000)] Recently, a California court of appeals court held that veganism was not a religious belief, providing no basis for religious discrimination by an employee who was denied work for refusal to take a vaccine grown in chicken embryos. [*See* "California Appeal Court Decides Veganism not Protected Religious Creed under FEHA," 19 *Employment Discrimination Report (EDR)* (BNA) 335 (Sept. 25, 2002)]

Similarly, in *Baltgalvis v. Newport News Shipbuilding, Inc.* [132 F. Supp. 2d 414 (E.D. Va. 2001)], a newly hired employee refused to give her employer her Social Security number for religious reasons. She contended that use of the Social Security number represented the "mark of the beast" as described in the Bible's Book of Revelation. In order to accommodate her religious convictions, she asked that another number be used to identify her in the company records. After she was terminated for refusing to provide her Social Security number, she sued, claiming violation of Title VII for the company's refusal to accommodate her religious beliefs. Recognizing as the court did that the IRS, and not the company, requires employers to provide the Social Security numbers of their employees, and provides penalties for failure to comply, the court found that the plaintiff failed to establish a case of religious discrimination under Title VII. In addition, the request for accommodation, the court concluded, would pose an undue hardship for the company, in that failure to comply with the IRS is a violation of federal law.

In *Mohamed-Sheik v. Golden Foods/Golden Brands LLC* [2006 WL 709573 (W.D. Ky. March 16, 2006)], the court, finding numerous precedent for the proposition that employers are not obligated to accommodate a religious concern when doing so would potentially create a safety risk, remanded the case to the trial court to determine whether such a risk was present in connection with a claimed policy that required employees to tuck in their shirts, which the discharged employee contended was against her religious beliefs.

Gender-Based Discrimination

Q 4:58.1   Is it reverse discrimination to treat biological mothers and fathers differently in disability leave policies?

Although one typically views Title VII sex discrimination claims as claims of illegal discrimination mounted by women, so-called reverse discrimination claims are cognizable under Title VII. In *Johnson v. University of Iowa* [431 F.3d 325 (8th Cir. 2005)], a biological father brought a class action challenging a public university's parental leave policy that allowed biological mothers to use accumulated sick leave upon the arrival of a new child but did not extend the same benefit to biological fathers. Although it would appear that the policy on its face was discriminatory, the court, in analyzing the policy, concluded that the sick leave was more akin to disability leave, as opposed to leave to care for the newborn, which could be used by both the biological mother and the biological father. However, having found the leave more akin to disability leave, and the fact that the biological father obviously did not go through the physical trauma of labor, this was a distinguishing characteristic between the biological mother and the biological father, which prevented the biological father from establishing a prima facie case under Title VII. Simply put, he could not argue that he was "similarly situated" to the mother for purposes of Title VII analysis.

Q 4:67.1   Does an employee have to be pregnant to maintain a claim under the Pregnancy Discrimination Act?

Although it would seem logical to presume that an employee must be pregnant to be able to make claims under the Pregnancy Discrimination Act, such is not necessarily the case. The U.S. Supreme Court, some time ago, held that the Pregnancy Discrimination Act prohibits an employer from discriminating against a woman "because of her capacity to become pregnant." [International Union v. Johnson Controls, Inc., 499 U.S. 206 (1991)] In *Kocak v. Community Health Partners of Ohio* [400 F.3d 466 (6th Cir. 2005)], a former employee claimed that her employer failed to rehire her due to a prior pregnancy that resulted in her resignation from employment. It was undisputed that the former employee was not pregnant at the time of her application for rehire, she did not bear any children during the period of her application, and no medical conditions related to pregnancy manifested themselves during the time of her application. Nonetheless, citing the Supreme Court's decision in *Johnson Controls*, the court held that if the former employee could produce sufficient evidence that the company refused to rehire her based on her "potential pregnancy," a case under the Pregnancy Discrimination Act would stand. However, the court in reviewing the evidence found that the former employee provided no such direct or circumstantial evidence to withstand a motion for summary disposition.

Q 4:67.2   Is harassment a recognized claim under the Pregnancy Discrimination Act?

As with other protected categories under evolving harassment law under both federal and most state statutes, a prima facie case of hostile work environment, harassment under the Pregnancy Discrimination Act, can be maintained if: (1) the employee belongs to a protected group (i.e., is pregnant); (2) the employee was subjected to unwelcome harassment; (3) the harassment comprising the complaint was based on her pregnancy; (4) the harassment was sufficiently severe or pervasive to alter the terms and conditions of employment and create a discriminatorily abusive working environment; and (5) there is a basis for holding the employer liable. [Walker v. Golden Pantry Food Stores, Inc., 2005 WL 3179988 (M.D. Ga.), citing Mendoza v. Borden, Inc., 195 F.3d 1238, 1245 (11th Cir. 1999)] In that case, the employee claimed that she had endured the alleged harassment for approximately one month and that the harassment included the following: (1) statements that pregnant people are "sorry" and "lazy"; (2) statements that she would not have been hired had the company known she was pregnant; (3) comments about the pregnant woman's uniform not fitting properly; (4) questions as to what the employee would do if she were to become sick; (5) company statements that the employee "wouldn't be here long"; and (6) "nit picking" the employee's performance. Recognizing that the Eleventh Circuit had created a relatively high bar for the assertion of hostile work environment claims, the court held that although the allegations indicated insensitivity and obnoxious behavior on behalf of the employer, the conduct was not sufficiently severe and pervasive to alter the terms and conditions of the employee's employment.

The Americans with Disabilities Act

Q 4:133.1   Is "interacting with others" a major life activity under the ADA?

One issue that courts have been struggling with is whether "interacting with others" is a major life activity under the ADA. [See, e.g., Doebele v. Sprint Corp., 168 F. Supp. 2d 1247, 1261 (D. Kan. 2001), which noted that the Tenth Circuit had not as of yet held "interacting with others" to be a major life activity.] This issue was recently addressed by the court in Price v. Facility Management Group, Inc. [403 F. Supp. 2d 1246 (N.D. Ga. 2005)] In Price, the employee suffered from bipolar disorder, a clear mental impairment, and claimed that his condition substantially limited his ability to interact with others, which he claimed was a major life activity under the ADA. Recognizing that the Eleventh Circuit has yet to decide whether "interacting with others" is a major life activity, the court held that even assuming that it is a major life activity, the employee had not demonstrated that it is an activity in which he is substantially limited. The plaintiff pointed to his difficulties in dealing with others and various outbursts to maintain the claim, but the court held that the record indicated that he was not "unable" to interact with others—he just occasionally did so in an inappropriate manner. As such, and without having to decide whether "interacting with others" is a major life activity, the court held that the employee's claim failed in this regard.

Age Discrimination

Q 4:147.1   Can acceptance of a voluntary early retirement plan be considered a "constructive" discharge in violation of the ADEA?

In *Embrico v. U.S. Steel Corp.* [404 F. Supp. 2d 802 (E.D. Pa. 2005)], the plaintiffs, former employees of the defendant, claimed that the Voluntary Early Retirement Program (VERP), which they accepted in Fall 2001 was not, in fact, a voluntary decision, but rather was coerced from them, such that the VERP violated the ADEA. In essence, all the plaintiffs claimed that they believed they had no choice but to resign and accept the VERP, and if they did not accept the VERP, that they would be terminated. As such, they felt they were compelled to resign and as a result, their resignation amounted to "constructive discharge." The court found that to demonstrate that the early retirement was involuntary, the court would apply an objective standard to determine whether a reasonable jury would conclude the employer permitted conditions so unpleasant or difficult such that a reasonable person would have felt compelled to resign. [Connors v. Chrysler Financial Corp., 160 F.3d 971, 974 (3d Cir. 1998)] The court reasoned that the situation must be so intolerable that a reasonable person would have felt he had no choice but to resign. Although all of the former employees believed that they would be fired if they did not accept the VERP, this conclusion was based upon the plaintiffs' subjective beliefs rather than on any clear information provided by the employer. The court found that the plaintiffs' general uncertainties to future prospects with the employer were not sufficient, and they must show that termination was objectively so certain that the plaintiffs had no choice but to retire.

Q 4:148.1   Can disparate impact cases be maintained under the ADEA?

In *Smith v. City of Jackson, Mississippi* [125 S. Ct. 1536 (2005)], the U.S. Supreme Court held that disparate impact cases (cases where illegal motive is not an issue), may be maintained under the ADEA contrary to the decision of many circuits that previously held that disparate impact theory was not cognizable under the ADEA. Disparate impact, as opposed to disparate treatment theory, has been recognized under Title VII since the U.S. Supreme Court decision of *Griggs v. Duke Power Co.* [91 S. Ct. 849 (1971)] In a case of first impression, the U.S. Supreme Court held in *Smith* that although the textual differences between the ADEA and Title VII make it clear that the disparate impact theory scope is narrower under the ADEA, it nonetheless exists as a theory of recovery under the ADEA. Specifically, unlike Title VII, if policies or procedures have a disparate impact in violation of the ADEA, it would nonetheless be acceptable, provided that the differentiation is based on reasonable factors other than age. In *Smith*, a number of police officers brought suit against the City of Jackson claiming that a pay plan that provided substantially greater increases of salaries for younger officers violated the ADEA. Although the Court concluded that the pay plan did, in fact, differentiate between the younger and older officers in terms of pay raises, the city defended its actions based upon its need to increase the starting salaries for junior officers to allow the city to compete with other similarly situated municipalities. This, the Court concluded, was sufficient for purposes of demonstrating reasonable factors other than age, and thus the city's pay plan was not in violation of the ADEA.

Q 4:149.1 What is a sufficient age discrepancy between a former employee and his/her replacement to maintain an age claim under the ADEA?

In *Oglesby v. Hy-Vee, Inc.* [402 F. Supp. 2d 1296 (D. Ct. Kan. 2005)], the employer sought summary judgment based upon, among other things, the plaintiff's failure to maintain a prima facie case of age discrimination under the ADEA when the plaintiff was replaced by someone who was just five years and seven months younger. The court in *Oglesby* noted the U.S. Supreme Court decision of *O'Connor v. Consolidated Coin Caterers Corp.* [116 S. Ct. 1307 (1996)], which required that the plaintiff must show a "significant" age difference between him and the worker who replaced him to maintain a claim under the ADEA. The court then reviewed a number of circuit court decisions that came to a number of inconsistent results. [*See, e.g.,* Benjamin v. E. I. DuPont De Nemurs & Co., 75 Fed. Appx. 65 (3d Cir. 2003) (seven-year gap sufficient); Damon v. Fleming Supermarkets of Fla., Inc., 196 F.3d 1354 (11th Cir. 1999) (five-year gap sufficient); Carter v. Decision One Corp., 122 F.3d 997 (11th Cir. 1997) (three-year gap sufficient); Schlitz v. Burlington NRR, 115 F.3d 1407 (8th Cir. 1997) (five-year gap insufficient); Kitchen v. Burlington N. & Santa Fe Railroad Co., 298 F. Supp. 2d 1193 (D. Kan. 2004) (six-year gap insufficient); Housely v. Boeing Co., 177 F. Supp. 2d 1209 (D. Kan. 2001) (four-year gap insufficient)] After reviewing these conflicting decisions and recognizing the standard with which the courts treat motions for summary disposition, the court assumed, without deciding, that there was a sufficient age difference between the plaintiff and the worker who replaced him—five years and seven months—such that a prima facie case under the ADEA could be maintained.

Similarly, in *Whittington v. Nordam Group, Inc.* [429 F.3d 986 (10th Cir. 2005)], the Tenth Circuit was asked by the employer to reverse a jury verdict in favor of a former employee under the ADEA because the employer claimed that the five-year age difference between the plaintiff and the employee who replaced the plaintiff was not sufficiently "significant" under the U.S. Supreme Court decision of *O'Connor*, such that an ADEA claim could not be maintained. The court, after having reviewed relevant decisions and based upon its appellate standard of review, concluded that the five-year age difference was not sufficiently insignificant as a matter of law such that the age discrimination claim could not be maintained and affirmed the verdict.

Tax Issues

Q 4:157.1   If taxable, are the payments made to an employee in a Title VII claim subject to withholding taxes?

Certainly monies attributable to back pay and lost wages would be subject to withholding taxes. However, to the extent that the sums are attributable to something other than lost wages (i.e., emotional pain and suffering, costs, and the like), they would not be subject to withholding tax, although the sums would nevertheless be taxable. However, if the sums are not allocated in the award or settlement agreement, courts will typically find the sums allocable to lost wages for which withholding will be required from the award and/or settlement amount. Such was the case in *Rivera v. Baker West, Inc.* [430 F.3d 1253 (9th Cir. 2005)] At issue was the settlement of a Title VII claim alleging discrimination and wrongful termination. The parties entered into a settlement agreement that did not specify how the funds were to be allocated, but merely had the settlement amount, $40,000, to be paid less "required withholdings." Because the settlement agreement did not allocate the settlement to items that would not be considered wages, but referenced "less required withholdings" in the settlement agreement, the court concluded that the sums were for lost wages subject to full withholding.

The Equal Pay Act

Q 4:159.1   How do courts determine whether there is a violation of the EPA?

In *Kaplan v. Multimedia Entertainment, Inc.* [2005 WL 2837561 (W.D. N.Y.)], a television news reporter/anchor claimed that her employer had violated the EPA by paying her significantly less than a male television news reporter/anchor who performed substantially the same work. Although the court noted an annualized discrepancy of approximately $18,000, it nonetheless held that the media company was justified in the pay differential because of the additional 16 years of service that her male counterpart had with the company, noting that seniority is a legitimate factor to justify higher compensation under the EPA. However, in order to be justified, explanations of wage disparity must fit within the affirmative defenses under the EPA. In *Lewis v. Sheridan Broadcasting Network, Inc.* [2005 WL 2977799 (W.D. Pa.)], the broadcasting company attempted to explain the disparity between a female anchor's pay and a male anchor's pay based on market factors, but the court concluded that the company must produce evidence that the wage disparity in fact was created by a legitimate nondiscriminatory reason in order to obtain summary judgment. The company failed to do so, and the motion for summary judgment to the EPA claim was denied. In contrast, if the company can demonstrate that market pressures did in fact result in wage disparity, an EPA claim can be beaten. For example, in *Wernsing v. Department of Human Services, State of Illinois* [427 F.3d 466 (7th Cir. 2005)], the court held that in the agency's practice of paying transferees an initial salary equal to what they were earning in their old job plus a raise if that was possible under the pay scale for the new job, discrepancies resulting in female employees doing substantially the same job being paid less is not a violation of the EPA. As the court held, the Act does not require the agency to ignore market pressures in setting salaries for new hires.

Retaliation Claims

Q 4:161   Must the plaintiff have suffered an adverse employment action to maintain a Title VII retaliation claim?

In *Waters v. Home Depot USA, Inc.* [159 Fed. Appx. 943 (11th Cir. 2005)], the plaintiff filed a complaint alleging that her former employer, Home Depot, retaliated against her in violation of Title VII. After she was discharged from Home Depot, the plaintiff filed an EEOC complaint against Home Depot alleging discrimination. The plaintiff also purchased an interest in a cleaning services company that had a cleaning service contract with Home Depot. After the EEOC claim was filed, Home Depot terminated the contract with the cleaning services company. The plaintiff alleged in the complaint that Home Depot's termination of the cleaning services contract was done to retaliate against her for her pending discrimination charge. Although the court acknowledged that former employees may file charges of retaliation against former employers for retaliation attributable to post-termination conduct, in order for the charges to be actionable under Title VII's anti-retaliation provisions, the former employee must show he or she suffered an adverse employment action. Because the actions of Home Depot did not affect her employment, but merely her investment interests, the court held that the claim could not be maintained.

Q 4:162   Have the number of retaliation claims continued to rise?

As reported in the Sixth Edition, retaliation claims have increased over the years. According to the EEOC, retaliation charges have risen steadily from Fiscal Year 1992 (15.3 percent of all charges) to Fiscal Year 1999 (25.4 percent

Chapter 5

Personnel Files and Privacy Issues

This chapter explores the competing interests of the employer's right to compile and maintain information concerning its employees and the employees' expectations of privacy. The understandable desire of employees to protect their privacy and the equally understandable need of employers to protect their companies have created tension in the workplace. This chapter examines recent cases concerning these conflicting objectives.

Employee Privacy

Q 5:17.1 Can inadvertent and/or innocuous intrusions be actionable as an invasion of privacy?

In *Anderson v. City of Columbus, Georgia* [374 F. Supp. 2d 1240 (U.D. Ga. 2005)], the city operated a call center and notified operators at the call center that it would be monitoring calls. Call center personnel working the phones were provided headsets to use in the performance of their duties. After the recording system was installed, the call center operators discovered the system continued to record anything said into the headset while the telephone headset was off the receiver, even after a call was disconnected. In the case, after a call was disconnected, an operator complained about her boss, and the complaints were picked up by the recording and listened to by her boss, who then fired her for the disparaging comments. As to the claims of invasion of privacy under common law, the court concluded that in order to state a claim against the individual defendants, the plaintiff must be able to demonstrate that the recordings were an intentional intrusion upon the plaintiff's seclusion or solitude or into her personal affairs. To the extent that the intrusion was inadvertent and not intentional, a claim could not be maintained against the individual defendants.

Similarly, when an intrusion into a restroom is rather innocuous, under certain circumstances a claim for invasion of privacy will not stand. In *Williams v. City of Tulsa, Oklahoma* [393 F. Supp. 2d 1124 (N.D. Ok. 2005)], the city had equipped its underground collections department responsible for operating and maintaining the city's underground sewer system with an elaborate array of monitoring and surveillance devices and posted numerous signs warning persons in or about the facilities that the "premises [are] videotaped 24 hours a day." Although there were many issues in the case, the issue of invasion of privacy boiled down to alleged illegal surveillance in or about an office restroom. The camera at issue was not actually in the restroom, but pointed in the direction of the restroom door and could partially show the inside of the restroom only if the restroom door was propped wide open. Based on the limited nature of the intrusion, the court held that a tort for invasion of privacy could not be maintained as a matter of law.

Chapter 6

Security Issues

Protecting company assets is a significant concern for most employers. Employee theft is considered by many to be a significant problem generating a large percentage of business losses. But protecting assets involves more than just guarding against employee theft. As companies continue to expand their use of computer systems in connection with their business operations, information technology security issues are becoming increasingly important to businesses attempting to protect their information and information systems from theft or sabotage. An employer's assets are more than just money and property; they also include intellectual assets (e.g., trade secrets and confidential information) and the company's workforce. This chapter explores non-competition agreements and issues concerning their enforceability.

Non-Competition Agreements

Q 6:42   How do courts determine whether a restriction is reasonable?

The determination of whether a non-competition agreement is reasonable is a factually intensive analysis made on a case-by-case basis. In *Singh v. Batta Environmental Associates, Inc.* [2003 WL 21309115 (Del. Ch. Ct., May 21, 2003)], the court found that a two-year non-competition provision that prevented the former employee from competing within a 200-mile restriction was reasonable and enforceable: The time period was reasonable because it tracked the normal life cycle of the projects in which the employer was involved, and the 200-mile restriction was reasonable because it was tailored to include the area in which most of the employer's clients were located.

In *Pathfinder Communications Corp. v. Macey* [795 N.E.2d 1103 (Ind. App. 2003)], a disk jockey's prior employer sought enforcement of a non-competition agreement that, if read literally, would prevent the former employee from engaging in any work at various competing radio stations listed in the covenant. Although the court agreed that this restriction was overly broad, extending beyond the radio station's legitimate interests in preventing unfair competition, nonetheless, if the overly broad language contained within the restrictive covenant prohibiting the former employee from "engaging in activities" was deleted, the resulting language was sufficiently limited to render the covenant enforceable.

In *Bruce D. Graham, M.D., PA v. Cirocco, M.D.* [31 Kan. App. 2d 563, 69 P.2d 194 (2003)], a former physician of the employer had signed a non-competition agreement that provided that for a period of two years after the separation of employment, the physician would not solicit business within 150 miles of each of the employer's offices where the physician practiced and that the physician would not open an office for practice within a 25-mile radius of various hospitals, essentially prohibiting him from practicing in the entire metropolitan area. Reviewing the covenants at issue, the court found that the 150-mile non-solicitation provision was reasonable, but that the restrictions essentially barring him from practicing in the entire metropolitan area were excessive and unreasonable.

In *Comtech International Design Group, Inc. v. Price* [2003 WL 212230 (Mich. App. May 27, 2003)], an employee was subject to a preliminary injunction preventing her from violating a non-competition clause that prohibited her from working with any competitor within a 50-mile radius of the office or areas she was assigned to while working at the employer's office. Although she initially worked in competition with her prior employer at offices of a company located within the 50-mile range, she was later transferred by her subsequent employer to Florida, well outside the 50-mile radius. The trial court held that because her subsequent employer had an office within the 50-mile radius, she could not work for any other office of her employer, even outside the 50-mile range. On appeal, however, the court held that such an interpretation was too broad and would effectively bar the employee from working with her new company at any location in the world, clearly outside of what would be reasonable to protect her prior employer from unfair competition.

In *Quality Liquid Feeds, Inc. v. Plunkett* [2004 WL 2809865 (Ark. App. Dec. 8, 2004)], a feed supplier to the cattle and dairy industries sought to enforce a 2-year non-competition agreement with one of its former district sales managers. In the case, the court reiterated Arkansas' general principle that for a covenant to be enforced under Arkansas law, three requirements must be met: (1) the covenantee must have a valid interest to protect; (2) the geographical restriction must not be overly broad; and (3) a reasonable time limit must be imposed. Recognizing that under Arkansas law the restraints imposed by the covenant must not be broader than necessary to protect the covenantee's interests, the court upheld the lower court's determination that the above restriction was overly broad and unreasonable. Specifically, the court found that although protecting a principal's desire that a former employee not appropriate its customers is a protectable interest, the court found that the former employee had done nothing other than sell liquid feed since he graduated high school, that much of the customer information was either known by the former employee before he worked for the employer or could otherwise be compiled from general information, and the restriction would have a severe impact on the former employee's ability to earn a living.

In *Mowery Clinic, LLC v. Hofer, M.D.* [122 P.3d 838 (Kan. App. 2005)], the court held that a restriction that prevented a physician from engaging in any medical services within a defined area was unenforceable as written as there was no evidence the physician was in actual competition with his former employer. Similarly, in *Sharvelle, M.D. P.C. v. Magnante, M.D.* [836 N.E. 432 (Ct. App. Ind. 2005)], the court held that a covenant restricting an ophthalmologist from practicing "health care of every kind and nature" for a two-year period following termination of employment was unreasonably broad and unenforceable. As it relates to non-competition agreements involving doctors, in *Intermountain Eye and Laser Centers, PLLC v. Miller, M.D.* [127 P.3d 121 (S. Ct. Id. 2005)], the court acknowledged that restrictive covenants involving the doctor/patient relationship required greater scrutiny than restrictions contained in other types of agreements. In a departure from other jurisdictions, the Tennessee Supreme Court held, in *Murfreesboro Medical Clinic, PA v. Udom* [166 S.W.3d 674 (2005)], that covenants not to compete entered into by a private medical firm and a doctor violated Tennessee public policy and are unenforceable.

Q 6:43   How do courts determine whether injunctive relief is appropriate?

Generally speaking, absent a showing of irreparable injury, injunctive relief will almost never be granted. The determination of whether or not irreparable injury may occur depends on the facts of each case.

In *Ormco Corp. v. Johns* [869 So. 2d 1109 (Ala. 2003)], the Alabama Supreme Court held that, in determining whether an employer has demonstrated irreparable injury such that a preliminary injunction should be entered during the pendency of the litigation enjoining a former employee from competing in accordance with a non-competition agreement, the court held that a rebuttable inference of irreparable injury exists in cases where a former employee salesperson is actively competing with his former employer in the same geographic area in violation of a non-competition agreement. However, the employee can then rebut this inference by producing sufficient evidence that the competition of the employee will not irreparably injure the employer.

In *Supinski, M.D. v. Omni Healthcare PA* [853 So. 2d 526 (Fla. Dist. Ct. App. 2003)], the Florida District Court of Appeals upheld a preliminary injunction prohibiting a former physician from practicing within 10 miles of any of the employer's facilities and from soliciting the former employer's patients in accordance with a non-competition agreement. Although the physician argued, among other things, that he should be restricted only from practicing within 10 miles of the facility where he worked, the court found that the company's facilities were not widespread but were localized in one geographic area and that the restrictions seemed reasonably tailored to protect the employer from unfair competition. As such, the court found that the employer had established, among other things, a likelihood of success on the merits and affirmed the issuance of the preliminary injunction, enforcing the restrictive covenants according to their terms during the pendency of the litigation.

In *Montville v. Mobile Medical Industries, Inc.* [855 So. 2d 212 (Fla. App. 2003)], in the lower court, the employer succeeded in obtaining a temporary injunction during the pendency of litigation arising out of its prior employees' alleged violation of a non-competition agreement, conditioned on the employer's posting a $50,000 bond. The former employees appealed, alleging that the bond should be significantly higher as they stood to lose over $400,000 if the employer was not successful at trial. Reviewing the facts, and noting that it appears likely that the court properly took into consideration the unlikelihood of the former employees overturning the temporary injunction, the court concluded that there was no clear abuse of discretion by the trial court.

In *Merrill, Lynch, Pierce, Fenner & Smith, Inc. v. McClafferty* [287 F. Supp. 2d 1244 (D. Haw. 2003)], a securities brokerage firm demonstrated that it would be irreparably harmed absent a temporary restraining order during the pendency of the litigation, keeping a former financial advisor who had gone to work for a competitor from violating the covenants not to compete contained within an employment agreement.

In *D & W Diesel, Inc. v. McIntosh* [307 A.2d 750 (N.Y. Sup. Ct. 2003)], the court held that a restrictive covenant that covered a regional sales manager for a company in the business of selling hydraulic hoses was likely unenforceable because the manager did not possess any trade secrets or unique talents. In addition, the court concluded that any loss of sales occasioned as a result of a violation of the non-competition agreement could be adequately remedied in the form of monetary damages. Therefore, the prior employer failed to demonstrate the likelihood of success on the merits or that its damages were irreparable, such that the preliminary injunction entered by the trial court was vacated.

In *Downeast Mortgage Corp. v. Balzano* [2004 WL 1925525 (Me. Super., June 29, 2004)], a mortgage company sought a temporary restraining order during the pendency of the litigation to enjoin the former employees from breaching their respective non-competition agreements. The defendants were all former employees of the mortgage companies, had signed non-competition agreements, and all resigned and went to work in similar positions at a competitor. The mortgage company claimed that, absent injunctive relief, it would lose its good will and client base. Recognizing that injunctive relief requires irreparable injury, as opposed to injury for which monetary relief is available, the court concluded that any loss of good will or future economic injury arising from the former employees' work for a competitor can be calculated by evidence of past earnings on accounts and expert testimony such that damages can be awarded in terms of monetary relief, and that the allegations of irreparable injury are speculative. As such, the court refused to enter a temporary restraining order.

Under Illinois law, to obtain preliminary injunctive relief, the employer must show a protectable business interest in one of two ways: (1) by showing the former employee's use of confidential information, or (2) by demonstrating near-permanent relations with its customers, to whom the former employee would not have had access but for his or her employment with the employer. [Applebaum v. Applebaum, 823 N.E.2d 1074 (App. Ct. Il. 2005)]

In *Access America LLC v. Mazzotta* [2005 WL 2650093 (Conn. Super.)], the court upheld a temporary restraining order against a real estate agent who joined a competing firm within a 15-mile radius of his prior agency's office, in direct violation of the terms of the non-competition agreement.

Chapter 7

Job Safety

As this 2007 Supplement to the Sixth Edition went to press, the Occupational Safety and Health Administration (OSHA) was 60 percent of the way through its 2003–2008, five-year Strategic Management Plan. The plan's stated goals are to:

1. Reduce occupational hazards through direct intervention;

2. Promote a safety and health culture through compliance assistance, cooperative programs, and strong leadership; and

3. Maximize OSHA's effectiveness and efficiency by strengthening its capabilities and infrastructure.

The agency hopes to achieve these goals using the following tactics:

1. Direct intervention

    -   Maximize one-on-one interactions through more dynamic identification of targets and sectors.

    -   Meet agency goals through better targeting and innovative interventions.

    -   Work to abate specific hazards, such as lead and silica, and reduce amputations and ergonomics-related injuries.

    -   Reduce the rate of workday injuries and illnesses by at least 5 percent annually.

2. Culture of compliance

    -   Improve the collection and assessment of data to better understand where compliance assistance, leadership, outreach, and cooperative programs have the most impact.

- Enhance safety and health promotion, analyzing program effectiveness and developing new training and target areas.

- Add 125 new Voluntary Protection Program (VPP) and Safety and Health Achievement Recognition Program (SHARP) participants and 100 new partnerships and alliances.

- Increase annual participation in outreach and training programs by 10 percent.

- Complete an emergency preparedness plan.

3. Strengthened infrastructure

- Collect data in a timely and accurate manner.

- Improve monitoring of emerging issues, enhance measures of program effectiveness, increase collaboration with partners, and enhance customer communication.

- Ensure that OSHA staff have the necessary knowledge, skills, diversity, and capabilities to accomplish the agency's goals.

- Better manage human capital by addressing skills gaps, implementing a leadership succession plan, and developing better technical competencies while attracting and retaining the best talent.

Assessing its own performance in Fiscal Year 2005, OSHA released the following statement in 2006:

> OSHA enforcement remains strong and effective. In FY2005, following an explosion at a petroleum refinery, OSHA conducted the most extensive investigation of its kind which resulted in the largest penalty ever—over $20 million. Additionally, OSHA issued more willful violations during FY2005 than in any previous year. There are many components to OSHA's effort, and multiple intermediate measures of its effectiveness. However, the ultimate outcome measure of OSHA's effectiveness is the reduction in workplace injuries, illnesses and loss of life—the fact that more workers than ever before go home safe, healthy and whole to their families at the end of every workday.
>
> The Agency's Enhanced Enforcement Program (EEP) focuses on employers who, despite OSHA's enforcement and outreach efforts, repeatedly ignore their OSH Act obligations, and place their employees at risk. EEP targets cases with extremely serious violations related to a fatality or multiple willful or repeated violations. During FY2005, OSHA identified 615 inspections that

qualified as EEP cases—a 200 percent increase over the preceding year. The objective of EEP is to assure sustained compliance at these facilities. If an inspection is classified as an EEP, then it may receive, among other things, follow-up inspections, inspections of other workplaces of that employer, and more stringent settlement provisions.

In 2003, OSHA developed a 5-year Strategic Management Plan (SMP) directing the Agency's resources towards three over-arching goals, one of which focuses on the reduction of occupational injuries, illnesses, and loss of life. To accomplish the goals of fatality, injury, and illness reduction set forth in the Strategic Management Plan, OSHA identified seven industries with high injury/illness rates and a high proportion of severe injuries/illnesses for focused targeting of outreach, education and enforcement activity. These industries include:

- Landscaping and Horticultural Services
- Oil and Gas Field Services
- Fruit and Vegetable Processing
- Blast Furnace and Basic Steel Products
- Ship and Boat Building and Repair
- Public Warehousing and Storage
- Concrete and Concrete Products

During FY2005, OSHA conducted 2,924 inspections within these seven industries. Many of these inspections were a result of Local Emphasis Programs (LEPs), which Area and Regional offices develop to address specific hazards of their geographic location. The objective of our effort is to significantly lower the disproportionately high injury and illness rates in these industries.

Total recordable case rates continued their steady decline. The rate for 2004 (the most recent data available) was the lowest since the implementation of OSHA's revised recordkeeping standard in 2002. In addition to the decline in the rate of total recordable injuries and illnesses, the rate of cases that resulted in lost workdays fell yet again. The continued decline in the lost workday case rate means that fewer American workers encountered safety or health hazards that resulted in serious injuries or illnesses.

[http://www.osha.gov/dep/enforcement/enforcement_results_05.html]

OSH Act

Q 7:7   What is a *work site analysis*?

A *work site analysis* is a means of identifying hazards. It consists of regular safety and health inspections, a system through which employees can notify management about potential hazards without fear of reprisal, investigation of accidents and averted accidents, and identification of injury and illness trends with common causes. Employers may conduct work site safety and health surveys; analyses of facilities, processes, materials, and equipment; and routine job-hazard analyses to identify hazards.

To assist with the identification of hazards, OSHA provides a variety of on-line resources, such as the following:

- The Anthrax eTool (aimed at helping protect workplaces against terrorism) [http://www.osha.gov/SLTC/etools/anthrax/sampling.html]
- IIAR Process Safety Management Guidelines for Ammonia Refrigeration [http://www.osha.gov/SLTC/etools/ammonia_refrigeration/references/iiar_psm_guidelines.html]

OSHA also offers many more general materials to assist employers and employees, including the following:

- General Industry Quick Start compliance materials [http://www.osha.gov/dcsp/compliance_assistance/quickstarts/general_industry/general_industry.html]
- Construction-industry-specific Quick Start compliance materials [http://www.osha.gov/dcsp/compliance_assistance/quickstarts/construction/construction.html]
- A draft Model Training Program for Hazard Communication [http://www.osha.gov/dsg/hazcom/MTP101703.html]

Q 7:9   What should safety and health training encompass?

OSHA guidelines suggest that information employees need will vary, but that each employee should at least be informed about the general hazards and safety rules of the work site; specific hazards, safety rules, and practices related to particular work assignments; and actions the employee should take in the event of an emergency.

Safety and health training of supervisors should include the information employees need, as well as information about safety and health management responsibilities.

A wide range of training materials is available on-line or upon request from OSHA. These materials can be identified at http://www.osha.gov/pls/ publications/pubindex.list.

Q 7:19   Does OSHA provide any voluntary guidelines for employers seeking to improve their employees' working conditions?

Yes. In January 1989, OSHA issued voluntary guidelines that are appropriate for most employers. The guidelines are designed to encourage management practices that will prevent occupational injuries and illnesses. OSHA advises employers to establish comprehensive occupational safety and health programs that provide systematic policies, procedures, and practices. The voluntary guidelines do not apply to employers in the construction industry.

Among the guidelines available on-line or upon request from OSHA are the following:

- Voluntary Training Guidelines; Issuance of Revised Training Guidelines, 49 Fed. Reg. 30290 (July 27, 1984)
- Guidelines for Workplace Violence Prevention Programs for Night Retail Establishments (Standard Interpretations, Oct. 23, 1996)
- Revisions to the Voluntary Protection Programs To Provide Safe and Healthful Working Conditions, 65 Fed. Reg. 45649–63 (July 24, 2000)

[http://www.osha.gov/pls/oshaweb/searchresults.category?p_text= voluntary%20guidelines&p_title=&p_status=CURRENT]

Q 7:45   Which states have OSHA-approved health and safety programs?

The following 26 jurisdictions have OSHA-approved job safety and health programs:

- Alaska
- Arizona
- California
- Connecticut
- Hawaii
- Indiana

- Iowa
- Kentucky
- Maryland
- Michigan
- Minnesota
- Nevada
- New Jersey
- New Mexico
- New York
- North Carolina
- Oregon
- Puerto Rico
- South Carolina
- Tennessee
- Utah
- Vermont
- Virgin Islands
- Virginia
- Washington
- Wyoming

Note that the Connecticut, New Jersey, New York, and Virgin Island OSH Acts cover only public sector (state and municipal) employees. Also worth noting is that some states have supplemented their basic OSH Acts with emergency preparedness and homeland security initiatives. [*See* http://www.osha.gov/fso/osp/innovations.html#emergency (particularly the beginning of the "Examples of State Plan Guidance Materials" section).]

Examples of State Plan Guidance Materials

Q 7:57.1   What interagency cooperative efforts has OSHA undertaken?

Some examples of OSHA's interagency cooperative efforts include:

- Interagency development of a guidance manual for worker protection during hazardous waste cleanup and emergencies (Memorandum of Understanding; Dec. 18, 1980)
- General working relationships between OSHA and EPA Office of Pesticides and Toxic substances (Memorandum of Understanding; Jan. 19, 1981)
- Working relationship between EPA and DOL, specifically OSHA with respect to the requirements of section 9(a) of TSCA (Memorandum of Understanding; Feb. 6, 1986)
- Hazwoper EPA and OSHA jurisdictional issues (Standard Interpretation; Dec. 18, 1991)

- OSHA does not cover volunteers, but EPA does in Hazardous Waste Operations (Standard Interpretation; Feb. 12, 1992)
- OSHA's policy regarding the use of EPA-registered disinfectants (Standard Interpretation; July 15, 1999)
- EPA, OSHA, Update Asbestos Data (OSHA News Release; Sept. 14, 2001)
- OSHA and the Coast Guard join together to present the second New England Homeland Security Conference (OSHA Speech; May 27, 2004)
- Chemical Reactivity Hazards Management Alliance: Alliance Annual Report 2004–2005 (Aug. 4, 2005)

[http://www.osha.gov/pls/oshaweb/searchresults.category?p_title=&p_text =EPA]

Enforcement

Q 7:81.1   Does OSHA provide any assistance to help employers comply with the recordkeeping requirements?

Yes. OSHA provides assistance, including the following on-line resources:

- OSHA Publication 3169, "Do I need to fill out the OSHA Log of Work-Related Injuries and Illnesses?" brochure.
- Regulatory text for 29 C.F.R. Part 1904; recordkeeping forms; Recordkeeping Policies and Procedures Manual, Directive Number CPL 2–00–135; and Settlement Agreement: Occupational Injury and Illness Recording and Reporting.
- Contact information for actions to take if there is a fatality or catastrophe at the work site and regulatory text for 29 C.F.R. Part 1904.39.
- Documents containing the major changes between the old and new requirements and a side-by-side comparison between the two.
- Recordkeeping training presentations to assist presenters in discussing the OSHA recordkeeping rule at different levels.

[http://www.osha.gov/recordkeeping/index.html]

Penalties

Q 7:116.1   What is OSHA's policy regarding criminal penalties for workplace fatalities?

In 2005 OSHA issued new procedures for the investigation of workplace fatalities. These new procedures include the following guidance on criminal penalties:

A. Section 17(e) of the OSH Act provides criminal penalties for an employer who is convicted of having willfully violated an OSHA standard, rule or order when the violation results in the death of an employee. However, Section 17(e) does not apply to violations of the general duty clause. When there are violations of an OSHA standard, rule or order, or a violation of the general duty clause, criminal provisions relating to false statements and obstruction of justice may also be relevant.

B. The circumstances surrounding all occupationally-related fatalities will be evaluated to determine whether the fatality was caused by a willful violation of a standard, thus creating the basis for a possible criminal referral. The evidence obtained during a fatality investigation is of paramount importance and must be carefully gathered and considered.

C. Early in the investigation, the Area Director, in consultation with the investigator, should make an initial determination as to whether there is potential for a criminal violation. Refer to Chapter III.C.2.e, Criminal/Willful Violations, for additional information. The decision will be based on consideration of the following:

1. A fatality has occurred.

2. There is evidence that an OSHA standard has been violated and that the violation contributed to the death.

3. There is reason to believe that the employer was aware of the requirements of the standard and knew that he was in violation of the standard, or that the employer was plainly indifferent to employee safety.

   If the Regional Administrator agrees with the Area Director's assessment of the case, the Regional Administrator will notify the Regional Solicitor.

D. At the discretion of the Regional Administrator and the Area Director, and dependent upon Regional procedures in place, a Regional team or trained criminal investigator may assist in or perform portions of an investigation, as appropriate.

E. In addition to criminal prosecution under Section 17(e) of the OSH Act, employers may potentially face prosecution under a number of other sections of the United States Code, including, but not limited to:

- Crimes and Criminal Procedures, for actions such as conspiracy, making false statements, fraud, obstruction of justice, and destruction, alteration or falsification of records during a federal investigation
- The Clean Water Act
- The Clean Air Act
- The Resource Conservation and Recovery Act (RCRA)
- The Comprehensive Environmental Response, Compensation, and Liability Act (CERCLA)

[http://www.osha.gov/pls/oshaweb/owadisp.show_document?p_table= DIRECTIVES&p_id=3245]

Smoking in the Workplace

Q 7:160.1   Have any new laws or ordinances been passed to regulate smoking in the workplace?

A state-by-state summary of all regulations of smoking in the workplace can be found on the American Lung Association website. States that have some form of legislation restricting workplace tobacco use include:

Alabama	Alaska
California	Connecticut
Delaware	District of Columbia
Florida	Georgia
Idaho	Illinois
Iowa	Maine
Maryland	Massachusetts
Minnesota	Missouri
Montana	Nebraska
New Hampshire	New Jersey
New York	North Dakota
Oklahoma	Oregon
Pennsylvania	Rhode Island
South Dakota	Utah
Vermont	Washington
Wisconsin	

[http://slati.lungusa.org/appendixa.asp]

Workplace Violence

Q 7:235   What else is OSHA doing about workplace violence?

OSHA is funding a two-year, $200,000 study at the University of Maryland. The main purpose of the study seems to be a better understanding of the scope of the problem. Preliminary data indicate that workers most often victimized by workplace violence are:

- Special education teachers;
- Mental health professionals;
- Home health care workers;
- All-night convenience store clerks; and
- Cab drivers.

In making the award, OSHA indicated its intent to become a leader in "the new science of emergency preparedness."

OSHA provides employers with significant on-line materials with regard to workplace violence. These include:

- Information on applicable OSHA standards;
- Sources for learning more about dealing with workplace violence;
- Guidelines on prevention of workplace violence; and
- Training materials.

[http://www.osha.gov/SLTC/workplaceviolence/index.html]

Avian Flu

Q 7:249   What are the experts' predictions about avian flu?

The most dire prediction to date was made in the October 2005 issue of *National Geographic:* "Sooner or later a deadly virus that can jump from birds to people will sweep the globe." In an article titled "Tracking the Next Killer Flu," author Tim Appenzeller reported on the death of a Vietnamese child, then stated,

> Ngoan's death and more than 50 others in Southeast Asia over the past two years have raised alarms worldwide. Affected countries are struggling to take action; other nations are sending aid and advisers while stockpiling drugs and developing vaccines at home. And scientists have stepped up their research into the fateful traffic of disease between animals and people.

Appenzeller's article goes on to cite the opinion of Dr. Robert Webster of the St. Jude Children's Research Hospital in Memphis, Tennessee, who has studied flu viruses for some 40 years. "This virus," said Dr. Webster, "right from scratch is probably the worst influenza virus, in terms of being highly pathogenic, that I've ever seen or worked with." But, he added, "It can make that first step across [from bird to human], but then it doesn't spread easily from human to human. Thank God. Or else we'd be in big trouble."

Ultimately, the experts agree that we will "be in big trouble." The November 2005 issue of *Vanity Fair* concurred with *National Geographic*'s bottom line, stating flatly, "Every virologist we interviewed said the same thing: A pandemic will occur."

During the months following these in-depth and rather dire evaluations, avian flu has surfaced in parts of Europe, notably Eastern Europe and Turkey. Furthermore, strains of the flu are found to be occurring in an ever-increasing number of mammalian species.

Q 7:250   Has avian flu appeared in North America?

According to the Centers for Disease Control and Prevention (CDC):

> On February 19, 2004, the Canadian Food Inspection Agency announced an outbreak of avian influenza A (H7N3) in poultry in the Fraser Valley region of British Columbia. Culling operations and other measures were performed in an effort to control the spread of the virus. Health Canada reported two cases of laboratory-confirmed influenza A (H7): one in a person involved in culling operations on March 13–14, and the other in a poultry worker who had close contact with poultry on March 22–23. Both patients developed conjunctivitis (eye infection) and other flu-like symptoms. Their illnesses resolved after treatment with the antiviral medication oseltamivir.

> Although these are the only laboratory-confirmed cases of avian influenza A (H7) in humans during this outbreak in Canada, approximately 10 other poultry workers exhibited conjunctival and/or upper respiratory symptoms after having contact with poultry. Use of personal protective equipment is mandatory for all persons involved in culling activities, and compliance with prescribed safety measures is monitored. Epidemiologic, laboratory, and clinical evaluation is ongoing, as is surveillance for signs of avian influenza in exposed persons. There is currently no evidence of person-to-person transmission of avian influenza from this outbreak. For more information about this outbreak, visit the Canadian Food Inspection Agency website at http://www.inspection.gc.ca/english/anima/heasan/disemala/avflu/situatione.shtml

> In February 2004, an outbreak of highly pathogenic avian influenza (HPAI) A (H5N2) was detected and reported in a flock of 7,000 chickens in south-central Texas. This was the first outbreak of HPAI in the United States in 20 years.

> In February 2004, an outbreak of low pathogenic avian influenza (LPAI) A (H7N2) was reported on two chicken farms in Delaware and in four live bird markets in New Jersey supplied by the farms. In March 2004, surveillance samples from a flock of chickens in Maryland tested positive for LPAI H7N2. It is likely that this was the same strain.

In Spring 2006, as this Supplement was being prepared, a major federal effort was mounted in Alaska to examine thousands of birds, migrating from eastern and southeast Asia, in an effort to ascertain whether the flu is being carried to the North American continent by these migratory species, which wintered in warmer Asian climes.

Q 7:251   What travel recommendations are experts making with regard to avian flu?

The Marsh Higher Education Network, a subsidiary of the insurance-brokerage giant Marsh-McClennan, has issued the following guidelines for persons traveling to regions where outbreaks of avian flu have occurred:

- Avoid all direct contact with poultry; do not touch even healthy-looking chickens or ducks.
- Avoid poultry farms and bird markets where live poultry is raised, kept, and/or sold.
- As with all contagious diseases, frequent and careful washing of hands is strongly advised.
- Waterless, alcohol-based hand gels should be packed with luggage and used when soap and water washing is not readily available.
- All foods, especially those made with poultry and/or eggs, should be thoroughly cooked.
- If the traveler develops fever, difficulty breathing, and/or a cough, s/he should contact a U.S. consular officer for assistance in locating effective medical assistance.
- Upon return to his/her home country, the traveler should monitor for these same symptoms carefully for 10 days and consult a health-care provider immediately if any of them develop.

Q 7:252   What are OSHA's recommendations for farm and poultry workers and others at risk of coming into contact with avian flu?

OSHA offers the following guidance for farm and poultry workers and others at risk of coming into contact with avian flu:

1. All persons who have been in close contact with the infected animals, contact with contaminated surfaces, or after removing gloves, should wash their hands frequently. Hand hygiene should consist of washing with soap and water for 15–20 seconds or the use of other standard hand-disinfection procedures as specified by state government, industry, or USDA outbreak-response guidelines.

2. All workers involved in the culling, transport, or disposal of avian influenza-infected poultry should be provided with appropriate personal protective equipment:

   - Protective clothing capable of being disinfected or disposed, preferably coveralls plus an impermeable apron or surgical gowns with long cuffed sleeves plus an impermeable apron;

   - Gloves capable of being disinfected or disposed; gloves should be carefully removed and discarded or disinfected and hands should be cleaned;

- Respirators: the minimum recommendation is a disposable particulate respirator (e.g., N95, N99 or N100) used as part of a comprehensive respiratory protection program. The elements of such a program are described in 29 C.F.R. 1910.134. Workers should be fit tested for the model and size respirator they wear and be trained to fit-check for face-piece to face seal;

- Goggles;

- Boots or protective foot covers that can be disinfected or disposed.

3. Environmental clean up should be carried out in areas of culling, using the same protective measures as above.

4. Unvaccinated workers should receive the current season's influenza vaccine to reduce the possibility of dual infection with avian and human influenza viruses.

5. Workers should receive an influenza antiviral drug daily for the duration of time during which direct contact with infected poultry or contaminated surfaces occurs. The choice of antiviral drug should be based on sensitivity testing when possible. In the absence of sensitivity testing, a neuramindase inhibitor (oseltamavir) is the first choice since the likelihood is smaller that the virus will be resistant to this class of antiviral drugs than to amantadine or rimantadine.

6. Potentially exposed workers should monitor their health for the development of fever, respiratory symptoms, and/or conjunctivitis (e.g., eye infections) for one week after last exposure to avian influenza-infected or exposed birds or to potentially avian influenza-contaminated environmental surfaces. Individuals who become ill should seek medical care and, prior to arrival, notify their health care provider that they may have been exposed to avian influenza.

[www.osha.gov/dsg/guidance/avian-flu.html]

Q 7:253   What are the recommendations of the Centers for Disease Control and Prevention for health professionals with regard to avian flu?

The CDC offers the following recommendations for health care workers who may come into contact with avian-flu-infected patients:

All patients who present to a health-care setting with fever and respiratory symptoms should be managed according to recommendations for "Respiratory Hygiene and Cough Etiquette" and questioned regarding their recent travel history.

Patients with a history of travel within 10 days to a country with avian influenza activity and who are hospitalized with a severe febrile respiratory illness, or are otherwise under evaluation for avian influenza, should be managed using isolation precautions identical to those recommended for patients with known Severe Acute Respiratory Syndrome (SARS). These include:

1. Standard Precautions

   - Pay careful attention to hand hygiene before and after all patient contact or contact with items potentially contaminated with the respiratory secretions.

2. Contact Precautions

   - Use gloves and gown for all patient contact.
   - Use dedicated equipment such as stethoscopes, disposable blood pressure cuffs, disposable thermometers, etc.

3. Eye protection (i.e., goggles or face shields)

   - Wear when within 3 feet of the patient.

4. Airborne Precautions

   - Place the patient in an airborne isolation room (AIR). Such rooms should have monitored negative air pressure in relation to corridor, with 6 to 12 air changes per hour (ACH), and exhaust air directly outside or have re-circulated air filtered by a high efficiency particulate air (HEPA) filter. If an AIR is unavailable, contact the health-care facility engineer to assist or use portable HEPA filters to augment the number of ACH.
   - Use a fit-tested respirator, at least as protective as a National Institute of Occupational Safety and Health (NIOSH)-approved N-95 filtering face-piece (i.e., disposable) respirator, when entering the room.

Q 7:254   What are the CDC's recommendations for workers engaged in eradication with regard to avian flu?

The CDC makes the following, fairly extensive recommendations:

BASIC INFECTION CONTROL

1. Educate workers about the importance of strict adherence to and proper use of hand hygiene after contact with infected or exposed poultry, contact with contaminated surfaces, or after removing gloves. Hand hygiene should consist of washing with soap and water for 15–20 seconds or the use of other standard hand-disinfection procedures as specified by state government, industry, or USDA outbreak-response guidelines.

2. Ensure that personnel have access to appropriate personal protective equipment (PPE), instructions and training in PPE use, and respirator fit-testing.

PERSONAL PROTECTIVE EQUIPMENT

1. Disposable gloves made of lightweight nitrile or vinyl or heavy duty rubber work gloves that can be disinfected should be worn. To protect against dermatitis, which can occur from prolonged exposure of the skin to moisture in gloves caused by perspiration, a thin cotton glove can be worn inside the external glove. Gloves should be changed if torn or otherwise damaged. Remove gloves promptly after use, before touching non-contaminated items and environmental surfaces.

2. Protective clothing, preferably disposable outer garments or coveralls, an impermeable apron or surgical gown with long cuffed sleeves, plus an impermeable apron should be worn.

3. Disposable protective shoe covers or rubber or polyurethane boots that can be cleaned and disinfected should be worn.

4. Safety goggles should be worn to protect the mucous membranes of eyes.

5. Disposable particulate respirators (e.g., N-95, N-99, or N-100) are the minimum level of respiratory protection that should be worn. This level or higher respiratory protection may already be in use in poultry operations due to other hazards that exist in the environment (e.g., other vapors and dusts). Workers must be fit-tested to the respirator model that they will wear and also know how to check the face-piece to face seal. Workers who cannot wear a disposable particulate respirator because of facial hair or other fit limitations should wear a loose-fitting (e.g., helmeted or hooded) powered air purifying respirator equipped with high-efficiency filters.

6. Disposable PPE should be properly discarded, and non-disposable PPE should be cleaned and disinfected as specified in state government, industry, or USDA outbreak-response guidelines. Hand hygiene measures should be performed after removal of PPE.

VACCINATION WITH SEASONAL INFLUENZA VACCINE

Unvaccinated workers should receive the current season's influenza vaccine to reduce the possibility of dual infection with avian and human influenza viruses. There is a small possibility that dual infection could occur and result in re-assortment. The resultant hybrid virus could be highly transmissible among people and lead to widespread infections. Vaccination of all residents of affected areas is not supported by current epidemiologic data.

ADMINISTRATION OF ANTIVIRAL DRUGS FOR PROPHYLAXIS

Workers should receive an influenza antiviral drug daily for the duration of time during which direct contact with infected poultry or contaminated surfaces occurs. The choice of antiviral drug should be based on sensitivity testing when possible. In the absence of sensitivity testing, a neuraminidase inhibitor (oseltamavir) is the first choice since the likelihood is smaller that the virus will be resistant to this class of antiviral drugs than to amantadine or rimantadine.

SURVEILLANCE AND MONITORING OF WORKERS

1. Instruct workers to be vigilant for the development of fever, respiratory symptoms, and/or conjunctivitis (i.e., eye infections) for 1 week after last exposure to avian influenza-infected or exposed birds or to potentially avian influenza-contaminated environmental surfaces.

2. Individuals who become ill should seek medical care and, prior to arrival, notify their health care provider that they may have been exposed to avian influenza. In addition, employees should notify their health and safety representative.

3. With the exception of visiting a health care provider, individuals who become ill should be advised to stay home until 24 hours after resolution of fever, unless an alternative diagnosis is established or diagnostic test results indicate the patient is not infected with influenza A virus.

4. While at home, ill persons should practice good respiratory and hand hygiene to lower the risk of transmission of virus to others.

EVALUATION OF ILL WORKERS

1. Workers who develop a febrile respiratory illness should have a respiratory sample (e.g., nasopharyngeal swab or aspirate) collected.

2. The respiratory sample should be tested by RT-PCR for influenza A, and if possible for H1 and H3. If such capacity is not available in the state, or if the result of local testing is positive, then CDC should be contacted and the specimen should be sent to CDC for testing.

3. Virus isolation should not be attempted unless a bio-safety level 3+ facility is available to receive and culture specimens.

4. Optimally, an acute- (within 1 week of illness onset) and convalescent-phase (after 3 weeks of illness onset) serum sample should be collected and stored locally in case testing for antibody to the avian influenza virus should be needed.

Q 7:255   What are the CDC's recommendations for airline crews and airline workers, who meet inbound passengers, with regard to avian flu?

The CDC makes the following recommendations:

Many infectious diseases can be spread by human hands. Soiled hands are an effective means of delivering infectious material (e.g., saliva or other body fluids that may contain viruses) to the nose or eyes, where they can enter the body. Hand washing is an important way to reduce exposure to common infectious diseases. Cleaning one's hands with soap and water removes potentially infectious material from one's skin. Hands should be cleaned before preparing food, eating or touching one's face, and after handling soiled material (e.g., used tissues, lavatory surfaces), coughing or sneezing, and using the toilet. Waterless alcohol-based hand gels may be used when soap is not available and hands are not visibly soiled.

If airline personnel are ill, the following steps should be taken:

1. Avoid traveling.
2. Cover mouths and noses with a tissue or hands when coughing or sneezing.
3. Put used tissue in a waste basket.
4. Clean hands with soap and water or an alcohol-based hand gel immediately after coughing or sneezing.

PASSENGERS WITH SYMPTOMS OF POSSIBLE AVIAN INFLUENZA:
Management on a Conveyance

1. Personnel should be aware of the symptoms of avian influenza. Although experience with human infection is limited, persons infected with avian influenza would likely have fever and respiratory symptoms (cough, sore throat, shortness of breath). The cause of a febrile respiratory illness in persons who have traveled in areas where avian influenza is present is more likely to be a common respiratory illness, but such persons should be evaluated by a healthcare provider to be sure.
2. If flight crew members or other personnel are concerned that a passenger with symptoms of avian influenza traveling from an area with avian influenza may be infected, they should try to keep the ill passenger separated from the other passengers as much as possible (3–6 feet).
3. If the ill passenger can tolerate a mask, provide a paper or gauze surgical mask to reduce the number of droplets coughed into the air.
4. If a surgical mask is not available, provide tissues and ask the ill person to cover his or her mouth and nose when coughing and to put the used tissues into a wastebasket or bag.
5. If an ill passenger is unable to wear a surgical mask, personnel may wear surgical masks when working with the ill person.
6. Personnel should wear disposable gloves for direct contact with blood or body fluids of any passenger. However, gloves are not intended to replace proper hand hygiene. Immediately after activities involving contact with body fluids, gloves should be carefully removed and discarded and hands should be cleaned. Gloves should not be washed or reused.

7. The captain of an airliner bound for the United States is required by law to report the illness to the nearest U.S. Quarantine Station prior to arrival or as soon as illness is noted. Quarantine officials will arrange for appropriate medical assistance to be available when the airplane lands and will notify state and local health departments and the appropriate CDC officials. Quarantine officials will work with the airline and local and state health departments to assist with medical transportation of the patient upon arrival, disease control and containment measures, passenger and crew notification and surveillance activities, and airline disinfection procedures.

Management on Arrival

For Transportation Security Administration (TSA), Bureau of Customs and Border Protection (BCBP), and other personnel interacting with passengers arriving from areas with avian influenza, CDC does not recommend protective measures beyond those already in use for interacting with the general public.

1. As with other infectious illnesses, one of the most important preventive practices is careful and frequent hand washing. Cleaning hands with soap and water removes potentially infectious material from one's skin. Hands should be cleaned before preparing food, eating or touching one's face, and after handling soiled material (e.g., used tissues, lavatory surfaces), coughing or sneezing, and using the toilet. Waterless alcohol-based hand gels may be used when soap is not available and hands are not visibly soiled.

2. Personnel who have to detain or assist a passenger who appears to have a respiratory illness and who may have traveled from an area with avian influenza should try to keep the ill passenger separated from the other passengers as much as possible (3–6 feet), and should immediately contact the appropriate authorities, such as the U.S. Quarantine Station with local jurisdiction and Emergency Medical Services (EMS).

3. While waiting for EMS or authorities to respond, provide the ill passenger with a gauze or paper surgical mask to reduce the number of droplets coughed into the air.

4. If a surgical mask is not available, provide tissues and ask the ill person to cover his or her mouth and nose when coughing and to put the used tissues into a waste basket or bag. If the ill passenger is unable to wear a surgical mask, personnel may wear surgical masks when in contact with the ill person (3 feet or closer).

5. Personnel should wear disposable gloves if touching blood or body fluids. However, gloves are not intended to replace proper hand hygiene. Immediately after activities involving contact with body fluids, gloves should be carefully removed and discarded and hands should be cleaned with soap and water or an alcohol based hand gel (if hands are not visibly soiled). Gloves should not be washed or reused.

MANAGEMENT OF ILL CREW

Flight crew members and ground personnel who become ill and who believe they have been exposed to avian influenza should take the following precautions:

1. Do not travel while ill. Limiting contact with others as much as possible can help prevent the spread of an infectious illness. If crew members and ground personnel must travel (e.g., to seek medical care), they should wear a paper or gauze surgical mask to decrease the possibility of transmitting the illness to others.

2. If crew members and ground personnel become ill while traveling away from home, their employer should be notified and assistance should be requested in locating a healthcare provider. Employees should let their employer know if they are concerned about possible exposure to avian influenza, and ask about all available healthcare options.

3. If illness onset occurs while outside the United States, the U.S. embassy or consulate can provide names and addresses of local physicians.

4. Before crew and personnel visit a doctor's office, clinic, or emergency room, the healthcare provider should be warned in advance about possible exposure.

5. If illness onset occurs after return home, employees should contact a healthcare provider. Before going to the doctor's office or emergency room, the medical staff should be told about the employee's symptoms, the countries visited, and whether the employee had contact with poultry.

Chapter 8

Employee Compensation and Fringe Benefits

Employee compensation is a highly complex aspect of employment law involving legal wage restrictions that apply to a wide variety of occupations and compensation methods. This chapter provides updates concerning the Fair Labor Standards Act (FLSA) and new Department of Labor regulations effective August 2004.

Although employers generally are not required by law to provide fringe benefits to employees, there are many reasons for doing so. Fringe benefit plans give employers a competitive edge in attracting and retaining qualified employees. Once plans are established, employers must comply with legislative provisions that apply to their maintenance and the distribution of benefits.

Some fringe benefits are mandatory under federal law. The Family and Medical Leave Act (FMLA) requires covered employers to provide eligible employees as many as 12 weeks of job-protected unpaid leave during any 12-month period. This chapter discusses further developments involving the FMLA and provides information to assist employers in complying with its requirements.

Fair Labor Standards Act

Wages

Q 8:3.1   Are students who are required to perform chores as part of their curriculum at a boarding school required to receive wages under the FLSA?

In *Blair v. Wills* [420 F.3d 823 (8th Cir. 2005)], the court was asked to determine whether students at a private boarding school who are required, as a condition of their enrollment, to perform chores are in fact employees for which they should be paid FLSA wages. This was a unique situation in that the students who performed chores were not "volunteers" in the true sense because they were compelled to perform these duties in conjunction with their education. It was uncontested that the students were not paid for their work and that the work that was performed would typically be performed by janitors or other maintenance personnel who would typically be paid for their services. Nonetheless, the school argued that the chores at this private boarding school were an integral part of the educational curriculum and that the chores primarily benefited the students, not the school. Although the court found that by having students perform these chores, the school certainly defrayed costs that it would have incurred had it hired employees to perform these tasks, the court nonetheless concluded that the activities of the students did not make them employees under the FLSA. Thus, FLSA wages were not required to be paid.

Q 8:3.2   Do illegal aliens have FLSA rights?

In *Zavala v. Wal-Mart Stores, Inc.* [393 F. Supp. 295 (D. Ct. NJ 2005)], the court was asked to determine whether, in light of the U.S. Supreme Court decision in *Hoffman Plastic Compounds v. NLRB* [535 U.S. 137 (2002)], which held that illegal aliens did not have remedial rights under the NLRA, illegal aliens were afforded rights under the FLSA. Although Wal-Mart argued that *Hoffman* required the court to conclude that the individuals did not have rights under the FLSA, the court concluded that, unlike IRCA, a growing number of courts have found that illegal aliens are to be paid FLSA wages for work performed.

Hours Worked

Q 8:14.1   Are there any recent developments involving preliminary and post-work activities under the FLSA?

In *IBP, Inc. v. Alvarez* [126 S. Ct. 514 (2005)], the U.S. Supreme Court decided issues involving preliminary and post-work activities. At issue were the following: (1) whether time spent donning and doffing unique safety gear was compensable time worked under the FLSA, (2) whether the time spent by employees walking to their work stations after donning the special safety gear was compensable under the FLSA, and (3) whether the time spent waiting to don the special safety gear was compensable under the FLSA. Similar to the

Tenth Circuit, the court held that because the safety gear was unique and necessary for these workers to engage in their work, donning and doffing the special protective gear was an "integral and indispensable part of their principal activities," such that donning and doffing the special safety gear were working time compensable by the FLSA. Because it was integral and indispensable to the employee's work, any time spent walking to and from the production floor after donning and before doffing the special safety gear, as well as time spent waiting to don the gear, would also be covered by the FLSA. However, the court concluded that time spent waiting to don protective gear would not be covered under the FLSA.

Exemptions

Q 8:28.1   What happens if the employer has a practice of making improper deductions from salaried exempt employees?

Under the new regulations, if an employer has an actual practice of making improper deductions from salaried exempt employees, the exemption is lost during the time period in which the improper deductions were made for all employees in the same job classification working for the same managers responsible for the actual improper deductions. [29 C.F.R. § 541.603(b)] However, if the deductions are isolated or inadvertent, it will not result in a loss of the exemption if the employer reimburses the employee for the improper deductions. In addition, the new regulations contain a "safe harbor" that provides that if the employer maintains a clearly communicated policy that prohibits improper pay deductions, and includes a complaint mechanism for employees to report improper deductions and reimburses employees for improper deductions, the employer will not lose the exemption for any employees unless the employer willfully violates the policy. [29 C.F.R. § 541.603(d)]

Q 8:29.1   Are threats to dock pay sufficient to run afoul of the salary basis requirement for exempt employees?

Under both the old regulations, 29 C.F.R. § 541.118, and the new regulations, 29 C.F.R. § 541.602, in order to maintain a salary basis, the salary must not be "subject to reduction because of variations in the quality or quantity of the work performed." The issue of whether an employee's salary is "subject to reduction" was recently addressed by the Sixth Circuit in *Whisman v. Ford Motor Co.* [157 Fed. Appx. 792 (6th Cir. 2005)] In that case, exempt employees for Ford Motor Company claimed that Ford had violated the salary basis requirement by adopting a policy requiring its salaried employees to swipe their electronic identification badges to record their ingress and egress from the plant, and threatened that failure to do so could lead to possible "pay adjustments." Although there was no evidence that any salaried employee's base pay had ever been docked as a result of this policy, the employees argued that because the policy threatened pay adjustments, their salary was "subject to" reductions based on the quality or quantity of work performed. Citing the Supreme Court case of *Auer v. Robbins* [519 U.S. 452 (1997)], the court concluded that employees are subject to a reduction in pay when they are covered by a policy that permits disciplinary or other deductions in pay as a practical matter. That standard, the court held, would be met if there was either an actual practice of making the deductions, or if the employment policy creates a "significant likelihood" of such deductions. In this case, the court concluded that the threat did not amount to subjecting the salaried exempt employees to deductions as a practical matter and held that the policy and threatened pay adjustment did not defeat the salary basis test under the FLSA.

Compensation and Withholding

Employee Retirement Income Security Act

Q 8:112.1   How do courts determine whether there is an abuse of discretion by a plan administrator with discretion under the plan documents?

In *Belluardo v. Cox Enterprises, Inc.* [2005 WL 3078632 (6th Cir.) (unpublished decision)], newspaper carriers claimed that they were entitled to pension benefits under the newspaper's pension plan. At issue was language in the plan that defined covered employees as "any employee of the company except any employee . . . who is classified as a commissioned newspaper carrier under the company's personnel policy." Although newspapers historically have treated newspaper carriers as independent contractors and not employees, the newspaper carriers claimed that they did not fit within the exemption under the plan documents because there was no written "personnel policy" that classified them as commissioned newspaper carriers, in accordance with the terms of the plan documents. After determining that the plan documents provided the plan administrators with discretion, the court concluded that its review was limited to whether the plan administrators abused their discretion in interpreting the plan documents and concluded that the administrator's interpretation of the term "personnel policy" in the plan documents to include past practices in addition to written documents was reasonable and not an abuse of discretion. As such, the court found the newspaper carriers were properly excluded under the exemption contained in the plan as commissioned newspaper carriers who would not qualify for pension benefits.

In *Sherwood v. United Parcel Flexible Benefits Plan Short-Term Disability Plan* [156 Fed. Appx. 941 (9th Cir. 2005)], an employee who was denied short-term disability benefits challenged the decision under ERISA Section 502. When the employee made claim for benefits, she submitted various information concerning her reaction to various medications due to her chronic hepatitis, but the plan administrator was confused and sought further medical evidence to substantiate her report. When further information was not provided, the plan administrator denied the claim. Although the employee claimed that the administrator cherry-picked which information to consider and/or failed to request pertinent information, the court, finding that the plan administrator had discretion under the plan documents, concluded the administrator's insistence on additional evidence may not have been "the best or only way" in which the administrator might have exercised its discretion and found that exercise of discretion by the administrator was reasonable and that an abuse of discretion had not occurred. Similarly, in matters where plan documents provide administrators with discretion, this deference that courts provide to the decisions of plan administrators includes issues concerning the interpretation of plan documents. In *Colucci v. AGFA Corporation Severance Pay Plan* [431 F.3d 170 (4th Cir. 2005)], at issue was whether an employee's "first day" of employment with an employer under the plan documents for purposes of determining seniority and benefit payments was the employee's original hire date or the date the employee was rehired after resigning from the position previously. Although the plan itself did not contain an explanation, the court concluded that, in view of the discretion given to the plan administrator under the plan documents, the "first day" related to the date that the employee was rehired after resigning was not an abuse of discretion.

Q 8:114   Can beneficiaries or participants maintain claims under state law for damages caused by a misrepresentation by a plan administrator in connection with an ERISA benefit plan?

Section 514(a) of ERISA [29 U.S.C. § 1144(a)] preempts "[a]ny and all state laws insofar as they may now or hereafter relate to any employee benefit plan." The U.S. Supreme Court, in *Shaw v. Delta Airlines, Inc.* [463 U.S. 85 (1983)], held that Congress used the words "relate to" in the above section in their "broadest sense." As such, with few exceptions, state law claims, including those founded under state common law, are generally considered to be preempted by ERISA legislation, and recourse for beneficiaries and plan participants exists only under the prescribed bases for relief under ERISA. As such, common law state claims of fraud, misrepresentation, and the like against plan administrators for damages allegedly caused by misrepresentations were held to be preempted by federal law in *Juntunen v. Blue Cross Blue Shield of Michigan.* [No. 240266 (Mich. Ct. App. May 29, 2003)]

However, the Fifth Circuit joined a growing number of circuits that recognize the common law doctrine of equitable estoppel as a cognizable legal theory under ERISA for misrepresentations. In a case of first impression, the court in *Mello v. Sara Lee Corp.* [431 F.3d 440 (5th Cir. 2005)] concluded that equitable estoppel is available to an employee if the employee can establish (1) material misrepresentation, (2) reasonable and detrimental reliance upon the representation, and (3) extraordinary circumstances. In the *Mello* case, the employee demonstrated that she had been continuously told for some time that although she had been working with the defendant company for only a few years, her employer would credit her service date from the date she started with the prior employer that the company purchased. This representation was made continually, and the employee also received various illustrations informing her that her pension benefits would be based on the credited service date. However, the plan documents themselves were explicit that such crediting of her prior service would not be made, and as such, the court concluded that the plaintiff could not have reasonably relied upon the misrepresentations because the plan terms clearly provided that her prior service would not be credited in connection with determining her pension benefits.

State laws that apply broadly to health care institutions and health benefit providers but do not "relate" to an employee benefit plan are not preempted by ERISA. For example, in *Pharmaceutical Care Management Ass'n v. Rowe* [429 F.3d 294 (1st Cir. 2005)], a national trade association of pharmacy benefit managers brought an action seeking to enjoin enforcement of Maine's Unfair Prescription Drug Practices Act (UPDPA). The Act, among other things, made pharmacy benefit managers fiduciaries in relation to their role as middlemen in providing prescription drugs from manufacturers to pharmacies, and established a number of requirements that must be met by the pharmacy benefit managers. Although much of the work performed by pharmacy benefit managers clearly would have had some effect on drugs that may have been covered under a variety of employee welfare benefit plans, the court concluded that the pharmacy benefit managers were not fiduciaries, under ERISA, and that the law had no "connection to" or "reference to" an employee welfare benefit plan, such that preemption was not warranted. [*See* California Division of Labor Standards Enforcement v. Dillingham Constr., NA, Inc., 519 U.S. 316, 324 (1997)]

The Family and Medical Leave Act

Q 8:153   How is the FMLA enforced?

As is the FLSA, the FMLA is administered and enforced by the Department of Labor (DOL). Employees who believe the FMLA has been violated can file claims with the DOL. In addition, employees can institute private litigation to seek redress for violations. A private lawsuit must be filed within two years after the violation or within three years if the employer acted willfully.

Q 8:185   Are there any court decisions interpreting the FMLA and its regulations?

Sufficient time has passed since the enactment of the FMLA for court decisions to be reported involving the interpretation of the FMLA and its regulations as promulgated by the DOL. In January 1998, a federal judge ruled that language contained within the DOL regulations is unconstitutional. [*See* Seaman v. Downtown Partnership of Baltimore, Inc., 991 F. Supp. 751 (D. Md. 1998)] Specifically, the FMLA provides that to be eligible for family medical leave the employee must have worked for the employer for 12 months, performed at least 1,250 hours of service for the employer, and work at a work site where there are 50 or more employees within a 75-mile radius. In *Seaman*, the employer had granted an FMLA leave to an employee who was not eligible under the literal language of the FMLA because she had not worked for the employer for 12 months. During the leave, the employee was terminated and sued the employer, claiming rights under the FMLA. The DOL regulations provide that once an employer declares an employee to be eligible, whether he or she is or not, the employer is stuck with that decision and cannot "subsequently challenge the employee's eligibility." [29 C.F.R. § 825.110(d)] In addressing this situation, the court found that the employee was not eligible for FMLA leave and that the DOL did not have authority to extend eligibility, as envisioned, under the preceding regulation. ["Federal Judge Finds That Department of Labor Regulation Is At Odds With Plain Language of FMLA," 10(4) *Employment Discrimination Report (EDR)* (BNA) 107–08 (Jan. 28, 1998)]

The U.S. Supreme Court ruled that an FMLA regulation exceeded the authority of the Secretary of Labor by providing a categorical penalty against employees who fail to designate leave time as FMLA leave time. [Ragsdale v. Wolverine World Wide, Inc., 535 U.S. 81 (2002)] The regulation at issue [29 C.F.R. § 825.700(a)] provides that if an employee takes a paid or unpaid leave, and if the employer fails to designate the leave as counting towards FMLA leave, the leave does not count against the FMLA entitlement. In this case, the employee had taken 30 weeks of leave, clearly qualified for FMLA leave, but no designation by the employer had been made. Although the regulation section would require a different result, the Court held the regulation to be beyond the scope of the secretary's authority, rendering it unenforceable. The *Ragsdale* ruling was also followed by the Third Circuit in *Fogleman v. Greater Hazelton Health Alliance*. [122 Fed. Appx. 581 (3d Cir. 2004)] In that case, an employee who had not been advised of her FMLA rights had been on a leave that extended beyond 12 weeks. Following *Ragsdale*, the court found that in order to show prejudice, the employee was required to demonstrate that had she been advised of her FMLA rights, she could have returned to work after the 12-week period. However, the testimony in the case indicated that the employee was not able to return to her position at the expiration of the 12-week period, and as such, there was no prejudice for the employer having failed to provide notice to the employee of her FMLA rights.

In addition, numerous decisions emphasize the need of the employee to give adequate notice in order to receive protection under the FMLA. Generally, these cases involve situations where employers fire employees for absenteeism problems, and the employees claim that the absences were properly attributed to FMLA leave time, for which firing would be a violation of the FMLA. Although the regulations do not require the employee to articulate the words FMLA, it is incumbent upon the employee to provide sufficient information to the employer of a need for time off for a condition that qualifies for FMLA treatment. As such, if the employee does not undertake reasonable notice, no protection will be afforded, as seen in *Satterfield v. Wal-Mart Stores, Inc.* [135 F.3d 973 (5th Cir 1998)] In *Satterfield*, the employee was discharged for excessive absences over a three-week period. According to the facts of the case, the cashier provided little information for the reason for her absences, indicating on just one occasion that she would not be in on just "that [one] day" because she was sick. In reviewing the facts, the court found the information provided by the employee was insufficient for purposes of invoking protection under the FMLA. [See "5th Cir. Reverses $50,000 Award to Worker Who Gave Incomplete

FMLA Notice," 10 *Employment Discrimination Report (EDR)* (BNA) 285 (Mar. 4, 1998)]

If adequate notice is provided, courts are willing to award damages and penalties against employers who violate the FMLA, even if they are completely ignorant of the law. For example, in *Hayes v. Larry Klein Wholesale Meats & Provisions, Inc.* [No. 96 1592 CIV (D.C. Fla. Feb. 9, 1998)], a federal judge ordered a company to pay over $140,000 together with attorneys' fees and costs to an employee who had been fired after he notified the company that he would not be able to come in, so that he could care for his wife following surgery. [See "Man Awarded $140,000 After Being Fired from Missing Work to Care for Ailing Wife," 10(8) *Employment Discrimination Report (EDR)* (BNA) 251 (Feb. 25, 1998)] Similarly, in *Knussman v. Maryland* [No. B-95–1255 (D. Md. Feb. 2, 1999)], a state trooper was awarded $375,000 by a jury for his employer's refusal to grant him leave to care for his spouse and newborn. [*See* 12 *Employment Discrimination Report (EDR)* (BNA) 196 (Feb. 10, 1999)] In *Armstead v. Caesars Atlantic Hotel/Casino* [(D. N.J. No. 98-CV-4563)], a black-jack dealer was reported to have obtained a $500,000 judgment as a result of a termination in violation of the FMLA. [*See* 16 *Employment Discrimination Report (EDR)* (BNA) 23 (Jan. 3, 2001)]

In joint employment situations, the determination of the appropriate work site to use for purposes of determining whether the employer has 50 or more employees within 75 miles of the employee's work site can pose difficulties. Under the regulations promulgated by the Secretary of Labor, two entities may be considered joint employers when they both exercise some control over the work or working conditions of the employee. [29 C.F.R. § 825.106(a)] Typically, joint employment will be found to exist when a temporary agency supplies employees to another employer. Under the regulations in joint employment situations, the primary employer—the employer with the authority to hire, fire, make payroll and provide benefits—is responsible for providing FMLA leave, and the regulations further provide that it is the primary employer's work site that is used for purposes of determining whether or not the employee works at a work site with 50 or more employees within 75 miles. [29 C.F.R. § 825.111(a)(3)] However, this regulation posed difficulty for the Tenth Circuit in *Harbert v. Healthcare Services Group, Inc.* [391 F.3d 1140 (10th Cir. 2004)] In that case, a housekeeping service employee who regularly worked at a work site where there were fewer than 50 employees within 75 miles claimed that she was denied eligibility for FMLA leave in violation of the Act because her primary employer had more than 50 employees at its work site in another town. Her primary employer countered that it had no obligations under the FMLA because the work site where the plaintiff regularly worked was the appropriate work site to determine whether or not the 50/75 threshold was met. Although the regulations, if followed, clearly would have made the primary employer's work site the appropriate work site for purposes of determining whether or not the threshold was met, the court concluded that the regulations were invalid and constituted an arbitrary and capricious use of the Secretary of Labor's authority to promulgate regulations. The court reasoned that the 50/75 test was in place so as not to impose an undue burden on employers in providing leave and that to arbitrarily pick a work site other than the work site where the employee regularly worked, merely because joint employment was determined to have occurred, was inconsistent with the statute.

In addition to satisfying the criterion above having worked 1,250 hours during the previous 12 months, to be eligible, an employee must also have been employed for 12 months. The question of when an employer is to make the determination as to whether the employee has satisfied the 12 months requirement was faced by the Third Circuit in *Renart v. Chartwells*. [122 Fed. Appx. 559 (3d Cir. 2004)] In that case, the employee commenced employment on November 4, 1998, commenced her leave on October 26, 1999, and was terminated on November 5, 1999. Although she did not have 12 months of employment when her leave commenced on October 26, 1999, she satisfied the 12-month criterion as of November 4, 1999, the day before her termination. The employee argued that, because she was employed more than 12 months before her termination, her leave under both the FMLA and companion state law should have commenced as of November 4, 1998. However, the court, in reviewing the regulations, determined that the determination of eligibility for FMLA shall be determined "as of the date the leave commences." [29 C.F.R. § 825.110(d)] As such, because the employee had not been employed for 12 months at the time her leave commenced, October 26, 1999, she was ineligible for FMLA leave and leave under a similar state statute.

In *Brumbalough v. Camelot Care Center, Inc.* [427 F.3d 996 (6th Cir. 2005)], the court held in this case of first impression that, in light of specific damages listed in the FMLA and its regulations for violations—which do not specifically provide for emotional damages—emotional damages are not recoverable under the FMLA.

Q 8:186   What common mistakes do employers make with regard to the FMLA?

The following problems are representative of the types of mistakes employers consistently make in the administration of FMLA.

- *Failure to review eligibility criteria.* Covered employers under the FMLA must have 50 or more employees during 20 or more calendar workweeks in the current or preceding calendar year. Most employers are able to determine whether they are FMLA-covered employers without much difficulty; however, if they determine they are covered, they often do not recognize that employees also must meet eligibility criteria before the FMLA will apply. Specifically, to be eligible an employee must:
  - Have worked for the employer for 12 months (not necessarily consecutive),
  - Have performed 1,250 hours of service for the employer, and
  - Work at a work site where there are 50 employees or more within a 75-mile radius.

Many employers, once they recognize they are covered, assume improperly that all of their employees are covered by FMLA and routinely provide FMLA leave to people who are not eligible. This practice can pose numerous problems.

Example 8-3. An individual, prior to a leave, has performed 1,250 hours of service but has not been employed by the employer for 12 months. This employee is ineligible for leave, but the employer mistakenly tells the employee she is on an FMLA leave and starts counting time toward the 12-week allotment. Later, before the 12-week allotment is utilized, the employee returns to work and then meets the criterion of 12 months of employment with the employer, and then goes back on leave. At this point, the employee is eligible for FMLA leave, and if the employer denies leave for the full 12-week period, relying on mistaken FMLA leave in the past, the employer violates the FMLA regulations as they are written.

- As a result, employers need to make certain that before they attribute time to FMLA the employee must meet the eligibility criteria for purposes of utilizing FMLA time.

- *Failure to recognize time off as FMLA qualifying.* It is not unusual for employers to fail to allocate FMLA time to an employee's FMLA bank for many reasons. Generally, the situations involve an employee who does not specifically request FMLA time, but indicates to the supervisor the need for time off work as a vacation, personal day, or the like for circumstances that qualify as FMLA time. For example, an employee may be undergoing inpatient surgery the next week and would like to take vacation days to cover the surgery and recuperation. Although paid time-off benefits may be available, the time off would be allocated to FMLA leave for the period of absence necessitated by the surgery.

- *Failure to notify the employee of FMLA time.* Once an employer receives sufficient information to determine an individual is eligible for FMLA leave, it must notify the employee that the time off is being allocated to FMLA time. If an employer fails to notify the employee properly, the regulations provide that an employer may not retroactively allocate the time to FMLA time, even if the time off would be properly allocated to the employee's 12-week entitlement. [29 C.F.R. § 825.208] However, in cases where the employee cannot claim any prejudice as a result of such failure on behalf of the employer, the U.S. Supreme Court has held that the employee has no recourse under the FMLA. [Ragsdale v. Wolverine World Wide, Inc. 535 U.S. 81 (2002)]

- *Lack of diligence during certification process.* The regulations allow the employer to have a certification filled out by the relevant health care provider to determine whether the situation falls within the criteria established under the FMLA; however, simply sending a certification form is not adequate. The employer must monitor the situation to make sure that the information comes back, and if it does, that it is adequate for purposes of the FMLA. Employers are not permitted, once the health care provider has certified the condition as qualifying, to circumvent the certification by contacting the health care provider for more information. The employer is required to take it at face value unless it has reason to believe it is inaccurate. If it does, its only recourse is to have the employee examined by another health care provider, not affiliated with the employer, and at the employer's expense for purposes of certification. If the health care provider selected by the employer confirms the designation, the employer must abide by that designation. If confirmation is not made, the regulations provide that both the employer and the employee will select a third physician, in good faith, whose decision will be binding. If the parties cannot agree on a suitable physician and the employee fails to act in good faith, the decision of the health care provider selected by the employer will control. On the other hand, if the employer acts in bad faith with regard to the selection of a third health care provider, the determination by the employee's health care provider will control. In addition, the regulations prevent the employer from unduly harassing employees through the certification process when they are on FMLA leave and generally prohibits, absent extenuating circumstances, recertifications occurring more than once every 30 days. The certification provisions are technical and rigorous, and employers must understand them to ensure that they properly follow the regulations issued by the DOL.

- *Lack of training.* The FMLA is difficult to administer, and many of the problems that develop are a result of a supervisor's lack of understanding of FMLA policies and procedures. It is generally advisable that, in addition to office or HR staff, supervisors be trained to assist in identifying situations involving an employee's time off that may be allocable to FMLA. Training will make supervisors more knowledgeable of the FMLA allocation scheme and provide them the tools needed to assist in the implementation of an FMLA policy. Particularly in relation to allocating time off to FMLA, the supervisors in the field often obtain the notification and, if they are untrained, they will not spot vacation days, personal days, or other paid time off as FMLA-qualifying occurrences that can be allocated to each employee's FMLA bank under the regulations. As the regulations provide, employees need not request FMLA leave but merely communicate a need for time off for an FMLA-qualifying occurrence. The term "FMLA" does not need to be communicated.

Q 8:186.1   For what damages can an employer be liable if a violation of the FMLA is found?

An employer can be liable for the following damages if a violation of the FMLA is determined to have occurred:

- Lost wages/benefits;
- Interest on damages;
- Liquidated damages equal to lost wages/benefits; and/or
- Employment, reinstatement, or other equitable relief.

Q 8:186.2   Are emotional distress damages awardable under the FMLA?

The Sixth Circuit in *Brumbalough v. Camelot Care Center, Inc.* [427 F.3d 996 (6th Cir. 2005)] addressed the issue of whether emotional distress damages are recoverable under the FMLA. In what the Sixth Circuit determined was a case of first impression before the circuit, the court held that because the FMLA specifically lists the type of damages for which the employer may be liable and includes damages only insofar as they are monetary losses of the employee, such as salary and benefits and certain liquidated damages, the FMLA does not permit recovery for emotional distress.

Q 8:186.3   Is it a violation of the FMLA to deny bonuses for employees who use sick pay in conjunction with an FMLA leave?

In *Chubb v. City of Omaha, Nebraska* [424 F.3d 831 (8th Cir. 2005)], the court held that a city's policy of denying an annual leave bonus for an employee who used sick pay is not a violation of FMLA. The court reasoned that it was the employee's election to take the sick pay in conjunction with an FMLA leave, and as such, having elected sick pay, which is not required under the FMLA, the city could then deny the employee an annual leave bonus which is available only for employees who do not use sick pay during the year.

COBRA and HIPAA

Q 8:189.1   Is legal separation a qualifying event under COBRA?

Although divorce as a qualifying event is self-evident and needs little definition, the issue of what constitutes a legal separation such that a qualifying event has occurred under COBRA can be more problematic. For example, in *Simpson v. TD Williamson, Inc.* [414 F.3d 1203 (10th Cir. 2005)], the issue was whether protective orders entered by a court in a pending divorce action requiring the husband to "stay away from his wife" during their divorce action was tantamount to a "legal separation," thereby triggering COBRA notice requirements and the wife's corresponding obligation to pay premiums for continued coverage. In the case, the plan administrator considered the protective order a qualifying event, sent a COBRA notice to the wife, and, when the wife failed to pay COBRA premiums, terminated her coverage. Although not defined under the regulations or statute, the court noted that other courts that had reviewed the requirements of "legal separation" concluded that the term is uniformly understood to mean a formal, judicial alteration of the marital relationship. [*See Simpson* at 1205, citing Nehme v. INS, 252 F.3d 415 (5th Cir. 2001)] The court held that to constitute a legal separation, the separation must result from a judicial declaration of legal separation cognizant under state domestic laws. As such, the court concluded that the protective order was insufficient to create a legal separation under state law and, therefore, the

COBRA notice sent by the plan administrator was sent in error because a qualifying event had not occurred, and the wife's failure to make premium payments could not be used as a basis to terminate her coverage.

Q 8:190.1 After notice, how long do qualified beneficiaries have to elect COBRA continuation coverage?

COBRA provides that the election period must end no earlier than 60 days after the date the qualified beneficiary was notified of the right to continued coverage. [I.R.C. § 4980B(f)(5)(A)] However, it is important to note that the 60-day election period is not a maximum 60-day period set by statute, but rather is the minimum election period required by COBRA. This point was addressed squarely in *LifeCare Hospitals, Inc. v. Health Plus of Louisiana, Inc.* [418 F.3d 436 (5th Cir 2005)] In that case, the employer terminated the employment of a gravely ill employee and informed the employee's spouse of COBRA continuation coverage rights in or about July 2001, but coverage was not elected by the participants until December 2001, well after the expiration of 60 days. However, the court found that there was nothing in the plan documents that limited the election period to 60 days, but rather referenced COBRA which provides only that the election period be at least 60 days in duration after notice of COBRA continuation rights. As such, the court concluded that the December 2001 election was timely and required the provider to pay the employee's medical expenses.

Chapter 9

Government Contractors

The headline in the March 20, 2006, *Washington Post* reads, "Multiple Layers of Contractors Drive Up Cost of Katrina Cleanup." The story begins, "How many contractors does it take to haul a pile of tree branches? If it's government work, at least four: a contractor, his subcontractor, the subcontractor's subcontractor, and finally, the local man with a truck and chainsaw." *Post* writer Joby Warrick claims, "If the job is patching a leaking roof, the answer may be five contractors, or even six. At the bottom tier is a Spanish-speaking crew earning less than 10 cents for every square foot of blue tarp installed. At the top, the prime contractor bills the government 15 times as much for the same job."

In September 2005, in an effort to keep costs down, President Bush suspended the minimum-pay provisions of the Davis-Bacon Act, to the chagrin of organized labor. Nevertheless, as the *Washington Post* piece suggests, Katrina's damage comprised almost as large an opportunity for government contractors as the wars in Iraq and Afghanistan. The Department of Homeland Security captured the magnitude of this opportunity in a report issued in early 2006. The report can be found at http://www.dhs.gov/interweb/assetlibrary/katrina.htm.

As this 2007 Supplement goes to press, it may be fair to state that contracting with the federal and, to a lesser extent, state and municipal governments is the biggest opportunity presented to free enterprise in the United States.

Security Clearances

Q 9:2   What are the purposes of security clearances?

Personal Security Investigations (PSIs) and security clearances are intended to protect military intelligence and technology from threats posed by:

- Foreign intelligence services;
- Subversive organizations, such as terrorist groups; and
- Individuals susceptible to improper influences or who have records of dishonest conduct.

From the employee's perspective, a security clearance can really pay off. According to a story published in the *Washington Post* in early 2006, "Workers with a security clearance earn 24 percent more than counterparts with similar skills, according to a new survey that found Washington area workers earn among the highest salaries." The *Post* based its assertion on a survey that found that "the average cleared employee earns $65,684, compared with $49,650 for a counterpart without a security clearance. . . . Information technology management executives earn the most, $105,000." The survey went on to report, "Workers with clearances in Maryland, Virginia and the District earn among the highest salaries, $89,111, $77,108 and $70,072 respectively. . . . Those working in Iraq earn the most, $92,142." [www.clearancejobs.com]

Q 9:17.1   Are there resources available to help employers get security clearances for their employees or to locate employees who hold security clearances?

Some organizations ready and willing to provide this service include the following:

- Military.com—Military.com, a Monster company, helps employers find and reach qualified candidates with military experience. [www.military.com/Careers/EmployerPage/0,14544,,00.html?ESRC=msn_vethiring.kw&np=1]

- TAOnline.com—A comprehensive resource for government job seekers that contains job listings plus guidance on everything from resume preparation to security clearances. [http://taonline.com]

- About.com—This site covers a wide range of topics from home repair to military careers. Its military/government career pages include comprehensive information on security clearances. [http://usmilitary.about.com/cs/generalinfo/a/security.htm]

Affirmative Action

Q 9:27.1   Under the OFCCP's affirmative action plan requirements, which groups of employees must be covered?

Three groups of employees must be covered by affirmative action plans (AAPs):

1. Women and minorities [*See* Executive Order 11246; 41 C.F.R. Parts 60–1 and 60–2]

2. Individuals with disabilities [*See* Section 503 of the Rehabilitation Act of 1973; 41 C.F.R. Part 60–741]

3. Veterans [*See* Vietnam Era Veterans Readjustment Assistance Act of 1974; Veterans Employment Opportunities Act of 1998; Veterans Benefits and Health Care Improvement Act of 2000; Jobs for Veterans Act of 2002; 41 C.F.R. Parts 60–25 and 61–250]

Plans can be developed using the agency's template on the Internet at http://www.dol.gov/esa/regs/compliance/ofccp/pdf/sampleaap.pdf.

Q 9:27.2   What must the AAP cover with regard to each of the identified employee groups?

The AAP for women and minorities must be both retrospective and prospective. In other words, it should look back at the last year's data and inquire, "How well did we do?" and it should look forward and ask, "What should our firm do differently in the year ahead to improve the representation of women and minorities in those job groups where we have placement goals?" The women and minorities AAPs must contain the firm's analysis of its confidential and proprietary data relevant to answering these questions. In contrast, the AAPs for disabled individuals and veterans need not include data analysis.

Q 9:27.3   How many plans must a multi-location contractor prepare?

Each individual establishment employing 50 or more employees must have its own AAP. Smaller, stand-alone sites may either have their own AAPs or be a part of the plan prepared by the larger human resources unit responsible for that site or the plan prepared by the corporate official to which the site reports. So-called "corporate initiative employees" who are managed out of corporate headquarters can be counted either in the corporate headquarters AAP or the AAP of the separate location where the employee is based.

Q 9:27.4   Who are the employees for the purposes of the AAP?

Every employee to whom a corporation issued a W-2 is an employee for purposes of the data in an AAP. Expatriate employees are included and should be counted in the corporate headquarters' AAP. Aliens employed by the company overseas are not included. Temporary workers employed for three years or less or who are paid by a leasing agency or other third party may or may not be included in AAP data at the employer's discretion, even if there are a large number of them. Interns and co-op students, again, may or may not be counted at the employer's discretion.

Q 9:32.1   Of whom should the contractor be taking a data snapshot for reporting purposes?

Contractors should take a data snapshot for employees in the following categories:

- Applicants
- Hires
- Promotions and Transfers
- Terminations

Q 9:32.2   What information should be gathered on people in each of these data snapshot categories?

The following information should be collected for the data snapshot categories listed above:

- Race
- Gender
- EEO-1 classification category
- Hire date (if applicable)
- Annual salary (if applicable)
- Birthdate (usually used as a proxy for experience)
- Job title (if applicable)
- Physical location (if applicable)

Q 9:32.3   Are there any coding tips for compiling these data snapshots?

The following coding tips can assist in compiling the data snapshots:

- The snapshot can be taken at the close of the calendar or the fiscal year.
- Coding should be internally accurate and consistent across the corporation.
- Microsoft Excel's "Unmatched Query Wizard" (Microsoft Access) can help with a discrepancy check.

Q 9:33.1   How can a contractor develop its job group analysis?

Job groups are the centerpiece of any affirmative action plan. OFCCP and the EEOC currently recognize nine broad groups. The agencies plan to increase this number to 10 in the near future. Job titles can be obtained from the 2000 census codes. Smaller contractors may formulate their job groups according to the EEO-1 report. [*See* www.eeoc.gov/stats/jobpat/e1instruct.html]

A typical organization profile for purposes of job group analysis will use an organization chart and go department by department. Next, the contractor may do a salary sort, from lowest to highest, by department. In assigning each of these employees to one of the nine (soon to be 10) EEO job categories (groups), contractors should keep in mind that similarly titled employees may in fact fall into different job groups. Contractors should be particularly careful about employees with the generic title "project manager," which may mean more than one thing, even within a single organization.

Q 9:33.2   How can a contractor cross-check its job group analysis data?

When compiling job group analysis data, contractors should cross-check to ensure that the following conditions are met:

- All new employees hired during the last AAP reporting year and whose employment was not subsequently terminated during that year should appear in the year-end snapshot.

- All employees whose employment was terminated during the last AAP year, and who were not subsequently rehired by the company, should be excluded from the year-end snapshot.

- All new hires for the reported year should also appear as applicants for that year.

- All employees with hire dates in the reported year should appear on the hire list for that year.

- All employees with the same job title should appear in the same EEO category (currently nine, soon to be 10) (except that such generic government-contractor titles as "project manager" may require more precise parsing out of individual employees with that common title).

- All internal and external applicants should appear on the appropriate worksheets.

- No employee should appear more than once in a snapshot.

- Each employee should have a unique identifier (e.g., Social Security number, employee ID number).

- Particular care should be taken in correctly and consistently coding job title and race.

Q 9:33.3　How can a contractor use Microsoft Access to cross-check the company's job group analysis data?

When using Microsoft Access to cross-check its job group analysis data, a contractor can import relevant Excel files, including employees' unique identifiers (e.g., Social Security number, employee ID number). Contractors also should use the "Unmatched Query Wizard" function.

Q 9:34.1　How does a contractor set its placement goals?

The contractor can conduct the following analysis to set its placement goals:

- An external availability analysis will answer the threshold question: "What percentage of the labor pool, from which we draw applicants for the job titles we have included in each job group, consists of (1) women and (2) minorities?" The labor pool is the geographic region from which the company recruits for each job group. For executives and top professionals, this may be a national or even an international region; for blue-collar and clerical employees, the pool may be a single city or metropolitan region.

- Next, an internal availability analysis answers the concomitant question: "What percentage of the workforce consists of women and minorities who are available to us to potentially move into job groups by means of transfers and promotions?" This analysis will look at the feeder pools from which such transfers and promotions have historically occurred.

- Next, a two-factor analysis should answer the question: "Combining the internal and external categories of available women and minorities, what is the overall availability of these two groups in the overall labor pool?" An employer may want to give one factor or the other higher weight based upon a closer look at the prior year's employment transactions as compared with a longer historical perspective, which might indicate anomalies that occurred in the "snapshot" of the past year.

Q 9:34.2　Are there any tips about setting placement goals?

After the job group analysis, placement goals are the most important part of the AAP. The contractor should keep the following in mind when setting placement goals:

- Placement goals cannot be quotas—quotas are illegal.

- Legal counsel recommend using the so-called "80 percent rule," seeking to utilize in the composition of each job group the number of women and minorities that equals 80 percent of the percentage of women and minorities in the labor pool for that job group.

- Some companies use the "standard deviation" method, asking whether the percentage difference between the number of women and minorities in each of the company's job groups is significantly different from the percentage of women and minorities in the relevant labor pool.

- Labor counsel caution that almost any other method starts to look a lot like a quota.

Q 9:44.1 How aggressively has the OFCCP been carrying out its mission?

According to the international law firm of Morgan Lewis & Bockius, head-quartered in Philadelphia, "OFCCP's investigative and enforcement agenda has become more aggressive in the last few years." At the time this was written, the firm's labor lawyers forecasted 6,000 audits of government contractors in Fiscal Year 2006 (October 2005 through September 2006). The focus of these audits was so-called systemic discrimination in the areas of hiring and compensation.

Q 9:44.2 Are there new recordkeeping rules of which contractors need to be aware?

The Internet Applicant final rule, issued by the OFCCP, addresses record-keeping by federal contractors and subcontractors about the Internet hiring process and the solicitation of race, gender, and ethnicity of Internet applicants. The rule is the product of a lengthy deliberative process, including public input, to develop a definition of *Internet applicant* that is relevant in the Internet age (added to 41 C.F.R. § 60–1.3). The recordkeeping requirements of the rule (amending 41 C.F.R. § 60–1.12) are meant to provide meaningful data that OFCCP says it will use to enhance its enforcement of the nondiscrimination laws.

According to the Department of Labor website:

> The final rule [became] effective February 6, 2006, one hundred twenty days after the date of publication in the Federal Register. A contractor's recordkeeping practices must comply with the new rule on that date. For example, by February 6, 2006, a contractor must solicit demographic information about Internet applicants and retain the records required by the rule for hiring decisions made on or after that date. The rule does not apply retroactively to hiring decisions made before February 6, 2006.

[www.dol.gov/esa/regs/compliance/ofccp/faqs/iappfaqs.htm#Q1]

Q 9:44.3 What other obligations does a contractor have vis à vis OFCCP?

Contractors have the following obligations in relation to OFCCP:

- Filing of EEO-1 and VETS-100 forms
- Posting requisite EEO posters, the company's EEO and anti-harassment policies, and notice of the availability of the non-confidential parts of its AAPs (usually made available in the HR offices)

Q 9:44.4 Where can a government contractor get more information and necessary forms?

The following on-line resources are available:

- OFCCP's website—http://www.dol.gov/esa/ofccp/index.htm
- EEO-1 Forms—http://www.eeoc.gov/EEO1/
- VETS-100 Forms—http://www.vets100.cudenver.edu

Additionally, a contractor can contact the Philadelphia law firm of Morgan Lewis for its OFCCP Alerts. [publications@morganlewis.info] On-line sources that can help find legal counsel capable of dealing with OFCCP and/or helping contractors comply include:

- LegalMatch—http://www.legalmatch.com/affiliate/index.html?affclk=0000150022&affId=150&AID=8261999&PID=1890979
- Legal Database—http://www.legalmatch.com/affiliate/index.html?affclk=0000150022&affId=150&AID=8261999&PID=1890979
- Lexis-Nexis/Martindale-Hubbell—http://www.lawyers.com/index.php?site=688&CMP=KNC-YAH

Q 9:44.5 How are contractors chosen for OFCCP audits?

According to the OFCCP, a combination of some 17 separate factors determines its selection of targets for audits. The most significant exercise conducted by the agency seems to be a comparison of the contractor's workforce profile from its EEO-1 form to the profiles of similar establishments in the same industry in the same region and with the labor market data from the 2000 census for that region. Companies with profiles dramatically different from their competitors and/or from the local labor pool are deemed most likely to present systemic discrimination issues.

OFCCP is developing its universe of government contractors both from self-identification on EEO-1 filings and from the Federal Procurement Data System, where even companies who failed to self-identify as government contractors on their EEO-1 forms will manifest as having federal contracts totaling $50,000 or more and, therefore, are fair game to the agency. A contractor can check whether it is on the Federal Procurement Data System at https://www.fpds.gov/.

Q 9:44.6 How will a contractor find out if the firm is the target of an OFCCP audit?

First, a Corporate Scheduling Announcement Letter (CSAL) is sent. The CSAL is a preliminary notice addressed to the company's CEO, alerting the corporation about which of its facilities are scheduled for auditing in the relevant federal fiscal year (October–September). OFCCP may or may not audit all the facilities targeted in the CSAL. The CSAL does not contain a precise schedule. Next, a 30-Day Scheduling Letter is sent. This is the contractor's actual audit notice.

Q 9:44.7 Can the company avoid an OFCCP audit after receiving a notice?

If the company believes that it is not a covered government contractor, or that certain specific facilities—such as those owned by a subsidiary—are not covered, it can challenge the OFCCP's jurisdiction. The government provides an on-line aid to making this determination at http://www.dol.gov/elaws/esa/ofccp/determine.asp.

This site contains some simple tests that will help you determine whether the targeted company and/or facility is covered.

Q 9:44.8 What is the OFCCP's focus in its enforcement agenda if the company is audited?

The OFCCP focuses on the following:

- Adverse impact of the company's hiring rules and practices and, to a lesser degree, its rules and practices for promotion and employment termination.
- The company's compensation practices; however, the agency's new standards on compensation are not yet final, so this aspect probably would not be pushed as hard as the hiring practices piece. All the same, almost all of the agency's regional offices currently use a rule-of-thumb approach toward triggering close scrutiny of a company's compensation practices. The relevant questions are as follows:
  1. Is the average difference in compensation between women and men 2 percent or higher?
  2. Is the average difference in compensation between minorities and non-minorities 2 percent or higher?
  3. Are 30 percent or more of women or minorities adversely affected by this difference?
  4. Is the number of women or minorities who are adversely affected by the compensation difference at least three times larger than the number of men or non-minorities adversely affected by the disparity?

Q 9:44.9 What should the company have ready for an OFFCP on-site visit?

In the event of an OFCCP on-site visit, the company should be prepared with the following documents and postings:

- I-9 Forms.
- Beck notices (see Q 9:66).
- Company's EEO policy.
- Company's anti-harassment policy.

- Federal six-in-one poster (must now include USERRA). Some sources of these posters include http://shopping.msn.com/specs/shp/?itemId=28705315,amp;fullDesc=1; http://www.ontimesupplies.com/Labor_Law_Posters_Human_Resources_subsection_224_page_1.html; http://www.shoplet.com/office/cgi-bin/categories.cgi?catid=5&sid=36&ssid=224
- Relevant state EEO posters, if any (see http://www.laborlawposter.us/)
- Notice of availability of AAP for viewing

Last but not least, managers should be prepared for interviews with OFCCP auditors.

Q 9:66.1 What new rules has OFCCP proposed?

The following are the names of the new rules being proposed by OFCCP and the necessary contact information:

- Affirmative Action and Nondiscrimination Obligations of Contractors and Subcontractors Regarding Disabled Veterans, Recently Separated Veterans, Other Protected Veterans, and Armed Forces Service Medal Veterans (01/20/2006)
- Affirmative Action and Nondiscrimination Obligations of Contractors and Subcontractors; Equal Opportunity Survey (01/20/2006)
- Affirmative Action and Nondiscrimination Obligations of Contractors and Subcontractors Regarding Protected Veterans (12/01/2005)

   This final rule revises the regulations implementing the affirmative action provisions of the Vietnam Era Veterans' Readjustment Assistance Act of 1974, as amended, 38 U.S.C. 4212 (2001) ("Section 4212" or "VEVRAA"). This rule makes three general revisions to the VEVRAA regulations. First, it generally conforms the VEVRAA regulations to the Veterans Employment Opportunities Act of 1998 (VEOA) and the Veterans Benefits and Health Care Improvement Act of 2000 (VBHCIA). Second, it removes references to letters of commitment because the violations formerly incorporated into the letter of commitment are now summarized in the Compliance Evaluation Closure Letter. Third, it removes language about the effective date of the rule published in 1998 because that language is obsolete.

   These regulations were effective January 3, 2006. For further information, contact James C. Pierce, Acting Director, Division of Policy, Planning, and Program Development, Office of Federal Contract Compliance Programs, 200 Constitution Avenue, NW., Room N3422, Washington, DC 20210. Telephone: (202) 693–0102 (voice) or (202) 693–1337 (TTY).

Wages and Benefits

Q 9:69.1 Where can a government contractor get wage determinations?

Wage determinations are available from the Wage Determinations OnLine website (www.wdol.gov).

Q 9:69.2   Are wage determinations ever unnecessary?

In the event of a national emergency, the president is empowered to suspend Davis-Bacon wage determinations and allow government contractors to pay lower than comparable regional wages. This occurred in September 2005 for the region hit hardest by Hurricane Katrina. In a letter notifying Congress of his decision, President Bush wrote, "I have found that the conditions caused by Hurricane Katrina constitute a 'national emergency.'"

Q 9:85   What is the Davis-Bacon Act's effect on state contracts?

Since 1931, the Act has been extended to control the prevailing wage requirements in some 60 related statutes that cumulatively provide federal assistance for construction projects via grants, loans, insurance, and loan guarantees. Some examples of such federal statutes, which serve as conduits of these funds to the states, are:

- Federal-Aid Highway Acts
- Housing and Community Development Act of 1974
- Federal Water Pollution Control Act

For more information on related state laws and issues, see the website of the National Association of Government Officials (NAGLO). [http://www.naglo.org/] NAGLO describes itself as follows:

> NAGLO is a professional association consisting of the chief official in each state and territory of the United States responsible for overseeing the laws that protect and serve working men and women throughout the nation. We strive to assist each member of the Association in the following ways:
>
> - By assisting members to develop a clear understanding of the issues they face on a daily basis, both in terms of sharing new approaches to common problems and by keeping members abreast of developments in Washington and the states;
> - By providing knowledge which will allow members to be better managers & leaders within their agencies;
> - By helping members establish a nationwide network of contacts with their peers to facilitate in the exchange of information; and,
> - By representing the views of state officials on important workforce issues, when the opportunity arises, in Washington.

Chapter 10

Public Employees

In 2005, most states were emerging from three successive years of budget deficits. However, budgetary challenges remained significant. According to the American Federation of State, County and Municipal Employees (AFSCME), "Medicaid and education are the fastest growing expenditures for state and local governments." At the federal level, the President's 2006 budget proposed shifting some $60 billion in Medicaid costs onto the states over the next decade. States also faced the prospect of decreased federal spending in the area of education, where $1.3 billion was on the block in the Bush administration's 2006 proposal. Cuts included Drug-Free Schools State Grants, Education Technology State Grants, and the Even Start literacy program.

The only region to see significant increases in federal support for state and municipal government needs is the Gulf of Mexico, where the devastation wrought by Hurricane Katrina requires—and continues to require—large infusions of federal funds to assist in the massive rebuilding effort.

Everywhere else, as pointed out in the Winter 2005 issue of *The Public Manager*,

> States currently face a fiscal situation remarkably similar to the downturns of the early 1980s and 1990s. A boiling economy led to booming state budgets. As the cyclical economic tide ebbed, state revenues faded too. Simultaneously, spending pressures, particularly Medicaid and other health care costs, squeezed states tightly. States have responded by cutting budgets dramatically, drawing on reserve funds, and in some states, proposing the political hot potato of tax increases. More broadly, states are exploring the other types of short-term cyclical actions they can take and what sort of long-term structural changes they must make to ensure a greater sense of budget stability.

[Nick Samules, "Budget Instability in the States: Dilemmas of Process and Perception," The Public Manager, Winter 2005, www.thepublicmanager.org/articles/series03.htm.] This means, among other things, that public employers will continue to behave more and more like their private counterparts.

Similarly, other state and municipal agencies across the nation remain keenly interested in privatization of everything from schools to prisons as a means of reducing costs and injecting greater flexibility into their employment pictures.

Collective Bargaining

Federal Employees

Q 10:24　What are labor relations expected to look like under the National Security Personnel System?

According to the Department of Defense (DOD), labor relations under the National Security Personnel System will include the following principles:

- Requirement to bargain over changes to conditions of employment only when changes are foreseeable, substantial, and significant in impact and duration;

- Provision to bargain above the level of recognition at the discretion of the Secretary (national level bargaining);

- Provision to bargain with multiple units over a single issue, or set of issues, where installations or organizations have multiple bargaining units;

- Establishment of a National Security Labor Relations Board to resolve labor disputes;

- Retention of negotiated grievance procedures with arbitration; but excluding matters relating to pay, mandatory removal actions, and ratings of record (a separate administrative process for reconsideration of performance ratings will be established to ensure consistency in the way ratings are challenged); and

- Clarification of representation rights and duties.

The rationale is stated as follows:

> The proposed NSPS labor relations system is designed to recognize the Department's national security mission and its need to act expeditiously in executing its mission, while preserving the collective bargaining rights of its employees. The proposal expands non-negotiable management rights. It prohibits bargaining over procedures involved in exercising core management rights, but requires management to consult with unions— management must consider union views and recommendations but agreement is not required. [Defense Department] and Component-wide issuances (e.g., directives, policies, manuals) are non-negotiable. The proposal provides for bargaining over procedures to be used in exercising other management rights (e.g., layoffs, RIF, selection or promotion procedures, disciplinary actions), but such bargaining may occur post-implementation. The proposal provides for expedited collective bargaining with impasse resolution and does not restrict management's ability to act.

[*See* www.cpms.osd.mil/nsps/labor.html]

On February 27, 2006, a federal district judge examined the National Security Personnel System in the context of a challenge mounted by 13 labor organizations representing more than 350,000 DOD personnel. The court held that:

- The labor unions had standing to challenge the DOD regulations;
- The issue was ripe for judicial review, given that the unions' attack on them was grounded upon the theory that the regulations are illegal on their face;
- DOD and the Office of Personnel Management had satisfied their statutory obligation of collaborating with the unions;
- In establishing a labor relations system, the two federal agencies also had acted lawfully when they departed from the Civil Service Reform Act's chapter governing labor-management relations at the DOD, which pre-dates the National Defense Authorization Act;
- However, the new labor relations scheme established by the challenged regulations failed to ensure that the affected employees would be able to engage in collective bargaining;
- The National Security Labor Relations Board established by the new rules did not meet the congressional requirement for independent third-party review of the agency's labor relations decisions;
- The rule's process for appealing adverse agency actions fell short of providing affected employees with the fair treatment mandated by Congress; and
- Therefore, the offending portions of the new regulations ought to be subject to a permanent injunction.

[American Federation of Government Employees, AFL-CIO v. Rumsfeld, 422 F. Supp. 2d 16, 2006 WL 456725, 179 L.R.R.M. (BNA) 2082 (D.D.C.)]

The decision marked the second setback for the federal government in its effort to implement the new regulations. In August 2005, the same court ruled in favor of some 60,000 Department of Homeland Security employees, finding the following:

- The employees' unions once again had standing to sue;
- The unions' standing extended to the right to challenge the establishment of a Homeland Security Labor Relations Board;
- The plaintiff-unions also had standing to attack limitations on the jurisdiction of the Federal Labor Relations Authority and the Merit Systems Protection Board;
- The Civil Service Reform Act did not preclude pre-enforcement challenges of new regulations;
- The new regulations failed to ensure collective bargaining rights;
- However, the Department of Homeland Security did have the right to narrow the number of topics subject to bargaining and to establish the Homeland Security Labor Relations Board;
- Nevertheless, the sections of the new rules which sought to limit Merit Systems Protection Board jurisdiction unfairly restricted the board's powers of review;
- Therefore, the entire sub-part of the new regulations relating to labor-management relations should be permanently enjoined.

[National Treasury Employees Union v. Chertoff, 385 F. Supp. 2d 1, 177 L.R.R.M. (BNA) 3089 (D.D.C. 2005)]

According to the *Washington Post*, "The two court decisions mean the new systems at Defense and the Department of Homeland Security—each more than two years in the making, and affecting nearly 800,000 civilian employees—appear destined either for lengthy court appeals or time-consuming revisions."

[Christopher Lee, "Court Block's DOD's New Rules for Workers," Washington Post, February 28, 2006, at A01.]

Q 10:25　What is the Department of Justice's early retirement plan?

Approved by the Office of Personnel Management in April 2004, the DOJ's plan offers Early Retirement Incentives (ERIs) to some 600 employees. Part of DOJ's plan is to modernize the Executive Office for U.S. Attorneys; the hope is to bring in new blood to better support U.S. anti-terrorist operations. A particular target of the ERIs are redundant clerical workers whose tasks are now largely obsolete because computer-knowledgeable DOJ lawyers do much of the same paperwork on their own. ERI packages will range up to $25,000 each. In total ERIs were made available to:

- 250 lawyers;
- 275 paralegals/legal assistants;
- 50 secretaries; and
- 25 budget analysts.

Criteria were age 50 and 20 years of service, or 25 years of service with no minimum age restriction on applying.

On March 14, 2006, the Assistant Attorney General for Administration issued a memorandum detailing the criteria for DOJ early retirement under the Voluntary Early Retirement Authority (VERA):

> To be eligible for a VERA, you must have at least 25 years of creditable service (without regard to age); or be at least age 50 and have at least 20 years of creditable service. Additionally, you must have been continuously on the Department's rolls since December 7, 2005.
>
> For [the Justice Management Division (JMD)], the early retirement window period has been established as March 15, 2006, through March 31, 2006. Employees must declare their intention during this time period and separate no later than April 28, 2006. VERAs will be accepted on a first-come, first-serve basis; however, management retains the right to limit the number of voluntary early retirements . . . .
>
> Management has the right to establish new opening/closing dates if circumstances warrant. In addition, subject to changes in the staffing or budgeting situation, the JMD may need to further limit offers after this opportunity is announced.
>
> For this particular early retirement window period, VERA covers all JMD employees with the following exceptions:
>
> 1. Employees in the Operations Services Staff (OSS); however an opportunity to utilize VERA at a later date is planned;
> 2. Employees serving under time-limited appointments;
> 3. Employees who have not been continuously on the Department's rolls since December 7, 2005; and
> 4. Employees in receipt of a decision of involuntary separation for misconduct or unsatisfactory performance.
>
> At least the last five years of an employee's service must have been covered under the federal employee health benefits and life insurance programs in order to continue coverage under those programs in retirement. An employee under age 55 and covered by the Civil Service Retirement System will incur a penalty in the calculation of the annuity.

[www.usdoj.gov/jmd/ps/memvera03_17_06.htm]

State Employees

Q 10:28 How does a typical state statute balance public safety against the right of its employees to strike?

The Alaskan law is fairly typical of laws in the minority of states according state and municipal employees a limited right to strike:

1. It denies the right to "protective services" (i.e., police, fire, and paramedics);

2. It gives a limited right to utility, sanitation, and school employees;

3. It gives an unlimited right to other (i.e., non-essential) public employees.

An example of (1) is Pennsylvania's so-called Act 111, which denies police officers and firefighters the right to strike. To counterbalance this denial, Pennsylvania provides for binding interest arbitration regarding collective bargaining impasses. In order to accommodate this compromise, Article III, Section 31 of the Pennsylvania Constitution was amended in 1968, when the act was passed, to eliminate an express constitutional prohibition of such arbitration. Binding arbitration under Act 111 is conducted in front of a panel of arbitrators. Refusal by the loser to abide by the panel's award is subject to enforcement and appeal proceedings before the Pennsylvania Labor Relations Board. The process is exemplified by a recent case in which, "[f]ollowing the certification of the Teamsters union as the exclusive representative of a bargaining unit of county detectives the parties bargained to impasse for a CBA and eventually submitted the dispute to interest arbitration under Act 111. An arbitration panel subsequently issued an award that included increases in wages and benefits in excess of what the county unilaterally budgeted to pay the unit members. The county commissioners ratified the non-economic terms of the agreement, but rejected the economic improvements and unilaterally imposed a countywide wage and benefit package. A PLRB hearing examiner concluded the county's refusal to fund the award's financial portion for 2005 constituted an unfair practice in violation of Section 6(1)(a) and (c) of the PLRA." On appeal from the hearing examiner to the full board, the PLRB explained the differences between Act 111 and the Public Employee Relations Act of 1970, which applies to all other public employees in the Commonwealth.

> The County's arguments fundamentally fail to account for differences between interest arbitration under Act 111 and interest arbitration for . . . employees under the Public Employee Relations Act of 1970 (PERA). The legislative and constitutional history of Act 111 compared to that of PERA is instructive. In 1968 the General Assembly enacted Act 111 providing for "binding" interest arbitration for police and fire employees who otherwise were denied a right to strike in support of bargaining proposals. Because the Pennsylvania Constitution did not allow for binding arbitration, Article III, Section 31 of the Constitution was amended thirty-eight years ago to provide for "binding" interest arbitration for policemen, such as the County's detectives. In response to this well-established constitutional and legislative history, the County argues that it may, prior to the arbitration process, budget for wages for these employees and then refuse to comply with a binding award under the Constitutional and legislative scheme.
>
> In its exceptions the County makes no justification for its refusal to comply with the Constitution, legislative, and Supreme Court mandates to implement the Act 111 interest arbitration award. Instead, it argues the unfounded and self-imposed claim that legislative action is required to fund the award, and therefore it need not comply. First, this claim is not even viable for purposes of Act 111, Washington Arbitration Case, supra; City of Farrell v. Fraternal Order of Police

Lodge No. 34, 538 Pa. 75, 645 A.2d 1294 (1994), and therefore, the County's refusal to fund the Act 111 interest arbitration award for the County Detectives is, as a matter of law, an unfair labor practice in violation of Section 6(1)(a) and (e) of the PLRA, and the County's exceptions challenging the hearing examiner's conclusions in that regard are dismissed.

[Teamsters Local No. 764 v. Lycoming County, 37 Pennsylvania Public Employee Rept. 15 (PLRB 2006)]

Q 10:36   How is collective bargaining handled at the state and local levels?

A majority of states have provisions requiring, or at least permitting, some form of collective bargaining. Some statutes may use the term *meet and confer* rather than collective bargaining, but in actual operation the process is not substantially different from collective bargaining.

The scope of bargaining subjects may be restricted to protect the statutory authority of, or to ensure the provision of essential functions by, the public employer. Additionally, the public employer may be legally prohibited from agreeing with the union on particular subjects. For example, if state law requires a minimum number of evaluations of employees annually, the employer may not agree to a lesser number of evaluations.

Public sector labor relations statutes generally have broad management-rights clauses. As a result, the subjects of "wages, hours and other terms and conditions" of employment may be defined more narrowly than in the private sector under the NLRA.

The state PERBs generally classify subjects for bargaining into mandatory, permissive, and illegal subjects. *Mandatory topics* involve the narrowly defined matters relating to wages, hours, and other terms and conditions of employment. *Permissive subjects* generally are those related to government policy, the employer's function, or matters of management rights. *Illegal subjects* may include those matters to which the employer is precluded by law from agreeing. Some states may prohibit bargaining over certain terms that may be classified as permissive in other states.

Most states that allow public-employee collective bargaining mirror the federal scheme, as represented by the NLRA and enforced by the NLRB (see chapter 11), in the way they handle collective bargaining. Where one of the parties has negotiated in bad faith, or refuses to negotiate at all, the concept of "unfair labor practice" is a common remedy. For example, in a recent California case, the Public Employee Relations Board's

ALJ found that the employer-community college district violated [the Educational Employment Relations Act] provisions by unilaterally contracting out its police services to a municipality without providing the union with notice and opportunity to negotiate that decision. The ALJ

rejected the employer's argument that the charge was untimely and/or
that the union waived its right to bargain on the issue in question. The
ALJ issued a cease and desist order and directed the employer, upon
demand from the union, to restore positions in its independent police
services unit, to reinstate bargaining unit employees, and to rescind the
contract with the municipality. The ALJ also directed the employer to
make all affected employees whole for losses suffered as a result of its
unlawful action. The employer's conduct denied the union its statutory
right to represent bargaining unit members and interfered with bargaining unit members' right to be represented by the union, the ALJ
reasoned. The ALJ overruled PERB's holding in Barstow Unified School
District, 28 PERC 28068 [PERB 1997] (holding that union waived its
right to demand bargaining of subcontracting of transportation services
through contract language), to the extent it conflicted with his determination that the employer didn't establish a clear and unmistakable
waiver as a matter of law.

[Long Beach Community College District Police Officers Association v. Long
Beach Community College District, 30 Public Employee Rept. For California 16
(Dec. 13, 2005)]

Q 10:46   What are some recent examples of privatization in the public sector?

Some examples of recent developments in privatization, gleaned from
around the nation, include:

1. In late April 2005, Governor Jennifer Granhom of Michigan criticized the
   Grand Rapids Board of Education for privatizing busing of its students
   and for considering the contracting-out of custodial services. "Our
   experience is that privatization is not all that it's cracked up to be," the
   governor reportedly commented, adding, "In fact, I think we've
   demonstrated that we've done better bringing work inside instead of
   contracting it out." A spokesperson for Michigan's Office of Management
   and Budget expanded upon the governor's comments, contending that
   the state had realized savings of approximately $1 million in total by
   bringing back inside the system its child support call center and facilities
   management activities, both previously outsourced to private firms.

2. Also in late April 2005, the Florida House of Representatives—over the
   objections of Governor Jeb Bush, who accused the lawmakers of moving
   "beyond oversight into meddling"—passed a bill aimed at enacting tough
   new rules for state contracts. The statute, if eventually enacted, will also
   create a Commission on Efficient Government to monitor big-ticket
   outsourcing contracts.

   Meanwhile, Florida was poised to become the first state in the nation to
   privatize child welfare programs, having reached an agreement last year
   with a company called Our Kids of Miami-Dade and Monroe Counties to
   handle foster care, adoption, and child-welfare licensing operations across

the state in return for a $75 million annual fee. DCF Secretary Lucy Hadi, describing what has been the cornerstone of Governor Bush's plan to improve Florida's beleaguered child-protection system, stated, "The entire state will now benefit from qualified experts that are equipped to know the needs of their communities."

3. In California, in 2005, San Diego County moved to eliminate some 68 mental-health jobs, privatizing two outpatient clinics, as part of its effort to close a $14 million budget deficit.

4. In New York, the state's highest court heard arguments in 2005 on a decision by the Empire State to permit Empire Blue Cross and Blue Shield to privatize themselves to for-profit status in exchange for $2 billion worth of stock in the new entities. Half of the $2 billion windfall is earmarked for pay raises for state health care workers represented by the Service Employees International Union, which threw its weight behind Governor George Pataki's privatization plan for the health-insurance giant.

5. In Alaska, legislation was moving through the system in 2005 that would expand the pilot e-commerce project run by the state's Department of Transportation and Public Facilities' Southeast Region in 2004. Other state departments would be provided with this electronic outsourcing option if the new law is enacted. Critics contend the e-commerce idea in effect turns over purchasing duties to private firms that need not follow the same competitive-bidding rules that are imposed on the state's public agencies.

6. Nationwide, more than 40 percent of drinking water systems are privatized and regulated utility systems. Among the remaining 60 percent owned by local governments, outsourcing of water and wastewater services rose by 13 percent in 2001. The EPA estimates that over the next 20 years water and wastewater services will cost U.S. communities $300 billion to $1 trillion. Rising costs and eroding state and municipal budgets continue to push local governments to consider water privatization.

[Ted Balaker, "State and Local Privatization Trends," www.privatization.org]

7. The 2006 controversy over the proposed management of some U.S. port facilities by a company headquartered in the United Arab Emirates brought into the media spotlight the fact that "Numerous [U.S.] ports, airports, roads, water facilities [are] already run by foreign businesses. Approximately 80 percent of U.S. port terminals are leased and operated by foreign companies, including companies partially owned by foreign governments. Thirteen U.S. airports have management contracts with private companies, and all the companies have significant foreign ownership or involvement. Over 2,400 public U.S. water and wastewater systems are managed by private firms, many of which are owned by foreign parent companies. Foreign companies are leasing and operating U.S. toll roads in Chicago and Indiana . . . . Policy Analysts Leonard Gilroy and Adam Summers show how foreign-owned companies have

successfully owned and operated numerous 'critical infrastructure' systems throughout the United States for years."

[Privatization Center, www.rppi.org/privatization/index.html]

Q 10:51   What efforts have been made to limit teacher tenure?

A number of states have placed restrictions on teacher tenure:

1. Colorado, Florida, Massachusetts, New Mexico, and South Dakota have replaced the term *tenure* with terms such as *non-renewal contract* and *continuing contract*, but have retained many of the guarantees of continued employment on good behavior. [*See* Colorado Rev. Stat. Ann. § 22–63–203; Fla. Stat. Ann. § 231.61; Mass. Gen. Laws Ann. ch. 71, § 22–10–1]

2. Connecticut, Michigan, and New York have streamlined the process by which tenure can be rescinded and a teacher's employment terminated. [Conn. Gen. Stat. Ann. § 5–242; Mich. Comp. Laws Ann. § 3.91; NY Educ. Law § 3012]

3. Wisconsin has eliminated statutory tenure but permits collective bargaining of tenure-like protections. [Wis. Stat. Ann. § 118.22]

Notable legal attacks on teacher tenure and related contract rights during the past several years include:

- *Temple University fired longtime faculty member for incompetence*: Citing "neglect of duty and incompetence," Philadelphia's Temple University faced a legal challenge in Spring 2002 from a mathematics professor whom the school said refused to alter outdated teaching techniques in the face of administrative ultimatums. Although the president of the faculty senate stated that "(t)he administration at Temple scrupulously followed" its guidelines and the faculty union's president added that "(h)eroic efforts were made to work this out by all the players," the federal district court for Eastern Pennsylvania has allowed the professor's legal challenge to go forward to an upcoming jury trial. [Eisen v. Temple Univ., 2002 WL 32706 (E.D. Pa. Jan. 7, 2002); Robin Wilson, "Citing 'Neglect of Duty and Incompetence,' Temple U. Ousts Tenured Professor," *Chronicle of Higher Education*, Jan. 30, 2002] Although the union's president observed, "Forty years ago, a faculty member who wasn't concerned about student learning would have skated through with no problem," the fired faculty member retorted, "I am teaching kids who should not be in college, but I can't fail them. I can't use the same notes or same tests I gave in previous classes." The professor grounded his court challenge on federal and state constitutional rights, notably free speech and due process. Responding to the university's motion to dismiss, District Judge Ludwig denied the motion with regard to the plaintiff's First and Fourteenth Amendment claims, but granted the motion with regard to his state constitution count. Regarding the latter claim, the judge's opinion observed, "Plaintiff concedes that this claim should be dismissed because there is no private cause of action" under the Pennsylvania Constitution. However, the judge decided that the plaintiff's contention that the real reason for his firing was protests about other instructors' failure to complete required syllabi in the mathematics course in question was a sufficient allegation under notice-pleading rules to permit his First Amendment claim to be heard by a jury. Furthermore, although he started the action only when under a paid suspension and not yet stripped of tenure and fired, his suspension and pre-termination hearing allegations were "enough to raise due process issues," in support of his Fourteenth Amendment count.

- *University of South Florida fired tenured Palestinian professor for disruption*: In our age of videotape, Internet, and voicemail, it's wise to assume that our every word will be recorded and may someday come back to haunt us. In the case of Professor Sami Al-Arian, a 15-year faculty member at South Florida University in Tampa, that lesson hit home hard after 9/11. Also an Imam with his own mosque and Muslim school on the side, Dr. Al-Arian agreed to appear on Fox News' *The O'Reilly Factor* on September 26, 2002. He expected to speak about the peaceful side of the Muslim faith. Instead, he was questioned about alleged ties to terrorism. A month later, NBC's *Dateline* aired a segment that included a 10-year-old tape in which the professor said in Arabic, "Jihad is our path. Victory for Islam. Death to Israel. Revolution. Revolution until victory. Rolling to Jerusalem." Although he now explains these words away as symbolic and not meant to be taken literally, the university administration said that they led to threatening phone calls, directed mainly toward Dr. Al-Arian. Frightened reactions to the calls included the closing down of the computer science floor of the engineering building, where the controversial scholar had his office. He was placed on paid leave while, at the request of a university trustee, outside council concluded that he could be terminated under these disruptive circumstances. The case became the cover story of the *Chronicle of Higher Education* on February 8, 2002. One of the authors spoke with the dean of one of the colleges at South Florida. The dean confirmed that, "Yes, we sure had a story in the *Chronicle*. It is not easing down; in fact, things are still quite hectic—a lot of pressure on the president from both groups—those who favor and those who do not favor the firing. It is a tough spot to be in." The dean added, "Luckily, I have been out of this controversy, although my faculty are [among] the ones bearing the torch of academic freedom." Subsequently, the professor became the target of a federal indictment.

- *School board's buy-out of principal's employment contract was no violation of his due process rights*: Holding that a public employee has no separate, protectable property interest in the position itself, the Eighth Circuit held that the school board's buyout of the two years remaining on a plaintiff's employment contract satisfied all the due process requirements that constitutional law imposes on public employers. [Holloway v. Reeves, 77 F.3d 1035 (8th Cir. 2002)] Although the board did not provide the principal with notice and a hearing, the appeals panel was not persuaded that his Fourteenth Amendment rights had been violated. To the contrary, the court held that, because the employee's job was essentially a property right, payment of the two years of salary he would have earned had he been permitted to continue in the position met the full measure of the board's constitutional, as well as its contractual, obligation to the plaintiff.

> Our cases clearly establish that public employees are entitled to procedural due process when they are fired from positions in which they have a legitimate expectation of continued employment, that is, when the employee's entitlement to the job is sufficiently certain to amount to a constitutionally protected property interest.

Significantly, while clearly affirming this principle, the court went on to reject the plaintiff's contention that there existed intangible benefits which adhere to the holding of the position in and of itself—presumably such attributes as prestige, although the court did not speculate on what intangibles the plaintiff had in mind.

> We hold that there is no constitutionally protected property interest in a public policy-making position, aside from what are commonly called its economic benefits. Since Mr. Holloway's due process rights could not have been violated with regard to a non-existent property interest, the defendant board members are entitled to qualified immunity.

- In *Manila School District No. 15 v. Wagner* [2004 WL 308128 (Ark. Feb. 19, 2004)], the plaintiff had been hired as school superintendent on condition that she complete her supervisory certification within a time specified in her employment contract. Despite completion of the process by the end of year two on the job, the board met midway through that second year and declined to reappoint her. The plaintiff sued, alleging wrongful discharge, and amended the complaint to include sex discrimination when her replacement turned out to be a man. Concurrent with the amendment, she moved for an injunction to restrain the school board from proceeding with implementation of its hiring decision. She alleged irreparable harm to herself, and her lawyer got the trial judge to agree. The court of appeals punted the case to the state supreme court, since it was one of first impression. The Arkansas Supreme Court reversed the trial court, finding that no irreparable harm existed to support the injunction. Money damages for lost salary were sufficient to make her whole should she prevail, said the high tribunal. While not strictly a tenure case, the decision is worth noting since by analogy, loss of tenure might arguably also be compensable by money damages under similar circumstances—albeit, the analogy between a contract for specified term of years and the open-ended right to continued employment implied in tenure is imperfect.

- *In 2004, the Louisiana Supreme Court handed down a decision running against the perceived attack on tenure detailed in this answer. In Howard v. West Baton Rouge Parish School Board [865 So. 2d 708 (La. 2004)],* a tenured vo-tech instructor was fired after reporting the theft of a loaded gun from his wife's car, which he had borrowed and parked outside his classroom building. The school board first suspended him, then held a tenure hearing and terminated him. The trial court and court of appeals both upheld the board's decision. But the state supreme court reversed and reinstated him, holding that the facts of the case failed to establish "a rational basis supported by substantial evidence" for stripping him of his tenure and terminating his employment.

- *In January 2006, the University of Colorado announced that it would review tenure on all four of its campuses.* The announcement was timed to help defuse public and legislative criticism generated by a controversial tenured faculty member, Ward Churchill. Churchill had made national news headlines by suggesting in his published pieces that the victims of the 9/11 terrorist attacks on the World Trade Center deserved what they got, because they were serving an unjust capitalist system. Allegations of rape in the university's athletics program, which led to the president's resignation in summer 2005, also have kept the heat on the university system to institute some sort of "reforms." The university reportedly has hired a consulting firm and brought in a retired Air Force general to help drive the review process. [Piper Fogg, "Amid public scrutiny, the U. of Colorado reviews its process for awarding the coveted status," Chronicle of Higher Education, January 6, 2006, at A22]

Constitutional and Civil Rights

Q 10:60.1   What are the Department of Transportation guidelines on drug testing?

The Omnibus Transportation Employee Testing Act of 1991 requires drug and alcohol testing of safety-sensitive transportation employees in aviation, trucking, railroads, mass transit, pipelines, and other transportation industries. DOT publishes rules on who must conduct drug and alcohol tests, how to conduct those tests, and what procedures to use when testing. These regulations cover all transportation employers, safety-sensitive transportation employees, and service agents—roughly 12.1 million people. Encompassed in 49 C.F.R. Part 40, the Office of Drug & Alcohol Policy & Compliance (ODAPC) publishes, implements, and provides authoritative interpretations of these rules.

Q 10:60.2   Which alcohol screening devices are approved by the DOT guidelines?

- AK Solutions, Inc., Palisades Park, NJ: Alcoscan AL–2500, AlcoChecker, AlcoKey, AlcoMate, AlcoMate Pro, Alcoscan AL–5000, Alcoscan AL–6000.
- Alco Check International, Hudsonville, MI: Alco Check 3000 D.O.T., Alco Check 9000.
- Chematics, Inc., North Webster, IN: ALCO–SCREEN 02TM 2

- Guth Laboratories, Inc., Harrisburg, PA: Alco Tector Mark X, Mark X Alcohol Checker, Alcotector WAT89EC–1.
- Han International Co., Ltd., Seoul, Korea 3: A.B.I. (Alcohol Breath Indicator).
- OraSure Technologies, Inc., Bethlehem, PA: Q.E.D. A150 Saliva Alcohol Test.
- PAS Systems International, Inc., Fredericksburg, VA: PAS Vr.
- Q3 Innovations, Inc., Independence, IA: Alcohawk Precision, Alcohawk Elite, Alcohawk ABI, Alcohawk PRO.
- Repco Marketing, Inc., Raleigh, NC: Alco Tec III.
- Seju Co. of Taejeon, Korea: Safe-Slim.
- Sound Off, Inc., Hudsonville, MI: Digitox D.O.T.
- Varian, Inc., Lake Forest, CA: On-Site Alcohol 5

Q 10:60.3   Which companies sell breath-testing devices that are approved by the DOT guidelines?

- Alcohol Countermeasure Systems Corp. Mississauga, Ontario, Canada: Various
- BAC Systems, Inc., Ontario, Canada: Breath Analysis Compute
- CAMEC Ltd., North Shields, Tyne and Ware, England: IR Breath Analyzer
- CMI, Inc., Owensboro, KY: Intoxilyzer (numerous models)
- Draeger Safety, Inc., Durango, CO: Alcotest (numerous models)
- Gall's Inc., Lexington, KY: Alcohol Detection System—A.D.S. 500 and others
- Intoximeters, Inc., St. Louis, MO: Photo Electric Intoximeter; GC Intoximeter MK II; and others
- Komyo Kitagawa, Kogyo, K.K.: Alcolyzer DPA–2; Breath Alcohol Meter PAM 101B
- Lifeloc Technologies, Inc. (formerly Lifeloc, Inc.), Wheat Ridge, CO: PBA 3000B and others
- Lion Laboratories, Ltd., Cardiff, Wales, UK: Alcolmeter (various models)
- Luckey Laboratories, San Bernadino, CA: Alco-Analyzer Model 1000
- National Draeger, Inc., Durango, CO: Alcotest (various models)
- National Patent Analytical Systems, Inc., Mansfield, OH: BAC DataMaster (with or without the Delta–1 accessory)
- Omicron Systems, Palo Alto, CA: Intoxilyzer (various models)
- Plus 4 Engineering, Minturn, CO: 5000 Plus4*
- Seres, Paris, France: Alco Master
- Siemans-Allis, Cherry Hill, NJ: Alcomat
- Smith and Wesson Electronics, Springfield, MA: Breathalyzer (various models)
- Sound-Off, Inc., Hudsonville, MI: AlcoData
- Stephenson Corp.: Breathalyzer 900

- U.S. Alcohol Testing, Inc./Protection Devices, Inc., Rancho Cucamonga, CA: Alco-Analyzer 1000 Alco-Analyzer 2000
- Verax Systems, Inc., Fairport, NY: BAC Verifier (various models)

Q 10:68.1   Has the use of alternative dispute resolution of discrimination claims increased in the federal sector?

According to the EEOC's most recent Annual Report on the Federal Workforce (covering Fiscal Year 2004), "In FY 2004, ADR was used in 43.3% of all instances of EEO counseling, which represents an increase of 1 percentage point from the ADR participation rate (42.4 percent) in FY 2003. This increase may be due to an ADR offer rate that climbed from 73.0 percent in FY 2003 to 79.5% in FY 2004." The U.S. Postal Service was among the most avid users of ADR in the federal sector. According to the report,

> The U.S. Postal Service reported the highest ADR participation rate in the pre-complaint process (72.3%), whereas the government-wide average was 43.3% in FY 2004. The ADR participation rate is obtained by dividing the number of cases processed in ADR by the total number of instances of counseling. Agencies that had fewer than 25 cases processed in ADR were not included in the ranking.

Pre-complaint resolutions reportedly resulted in fewer filings in the federal sector, as well. The annual report also states,

> One of the purposes for pre-complaint resolution efforts is to resolve existing disputes early on to decrease the chances of future disputes between the parties. Although the EEO resolution rate (the sum of the total settlements and total withdrawals divided by the total completed counselings, see Table 4 in Appendix IV) decreased by 2.7% from FY 2000 to FY 2004, fewer individuals were counseled multiple times. *See* Figure 2. In fact, the number of individuals who sought counseling multiple times decreased from 10.6% in FY 2003 to 6.0% of all counselings in FY 2004. Consequently, resolutions at the pre-complaint stage have resulted in fewer formal complaints.

[www.eeoc.gov/federal/fsp2004/section1b.html#2]

Occupational Health and Safety

Q 10:96   In the wake of Hurricane Katrina, are there any state disaster plans that are deemed by OSHA to be models?

According to OSHA,

> Many of the OSHA-approved state plans have implemented or assisted in the development of emergency preparedness and/or homeland security related initiatives and guidance materials. These States cover most private sector workers and are also required to extend their coverage to public sector (state and local government) workers in the state.

Among plans cited by OSHA as models are:

California

- Workplace Security Publications [www.dir.ca.gov/dosh/puborder.asp]
- Guidelines for Security & Safety of Health Care and Community Service Workers
- Guidelines for Workplace Security
- Model Injury & Illness Prevention Program for Workplace Security
- Fact Sheet, Reducing Workplace Risks for Anthrax Exposures to Mail Handlers [www.dir.ca.gov/dosh/anthraxfinal3.pdf]

Oregon

- Expecting the Unexpected: What to Consider in Planning for Workplace Emergencies [www.orosha.org/pdf/pubs/3356.pdf]
- Oregon OSHA website links to sites containing information on bio-terrorism [www.cbs.state.or.us/external/osha/bioterror.html]

South Carolina

- Best Practices, Prepare, Prevent, Protect South Carolina, a "Workplace Security Guide designed to assist . . . in assessing [a] company's level of risk and to suggest ways to manage that risk" [www.llr.state.sc.us/workplace/workplacesecurity.htm]

Chapter 11

Labor Unions

The rights conferred upon labor unions and union employees are generally derived from the authority of the National Labor Relations Act (NLRA), which followed closely on the heels of the Norris-LaGuardia Act during the New Deal era of the 1930s. The NLRA is the "rule book" that labor organizations must follow when attempting to unionize companies that are covered by it. Likewise, an employer confronted with efforts to organize a union must be aware of the statutory mandates and prohibitions that apply to it as well as to the labor organization. The statute also governs the collective bargaining relationship after a group of employees has selected a union to represent it. This chapter provides information on developments in evolving areas concerning the NLRA.

Bargaining Units and Related Employment Practices

Q 11:39 Do unionized employees have a right to union representation in disciplinary matters?

Yes. Union employees have Weingarten rights (named for a famous NLRB case discussed below) that allow a union representative (e.g., a steward or an officer) to be present whenever an employee interview could lead to disciplinary action by the employer.

These so-called Weingarten rights have their genesis in the U.S. Supreme Court decision of *NLRB v. J. Weingarten, Inc.* [420 U.S. 251 (1975)] In interpreting the NLRA, the Court held in *Weingarten* that a private sector employee has a statutory right under the NLRA to refuse to submit, without union representation, to an investigatory interview that the employee reasonably believes might result in discipline. However, Weingarten rights do not extend to all circumstances where issues of an employee's performance are discussed with management.

In *In re Grievance of Vermont State Employees' Ass'n, Inc. and Dargie* [893 A.2d 333 (Vt. 2005)], the issue was whether a union employee was entitled to have a union representative present during two meetings she had with management where her performance deficiencies were discussed. Specifically, one meeting involved discussions concerning the employee's absences, and the other concerned the employee's lack of performance. Although performance issues were discussed, the court concluded that discipline was not meted out at any of the meetings, and in light of Vermont precedent—which prohibits the imposition of discipline if the employer fails to give the employee notice of Weingarten rights—held that lack of such notice from the employer necessarily made the employee's subjective belief that discipline might result from the meetings unreasonable. As such, no Weingarten rights were violated.

Chapter 12

Immigration and Naturalization

As this 2007 Supplement goes to press, immigration remains a hot topic, although the events of 9/11 are five years in the past. For example, President George W. Bush, in December 2004, signed twin reform statutes affecting the two most significant business-related visas available from the U.S. Department of State. Cumulatively, these reform measures:

1. Reintroduced a "training fee" into the H-1B application process. Rising to $1500 from the preceding $1000 tariff, the fee is intended to support a fund for retraining American workers displaced by H-1B alien workers.

2. Beginning March 8, 2006, dunned petitioners for H-1B worker visas a $500 "fraud prevention fee" payable to the U.S. Citizenship and Immigration Service (USCIS), one of two successor agencies to the INS. Both such fees are on top of the $185 application fee—$1000 for expedited handling.

In October 2004, the 65,000 available H-1B visas were snapped up like America's "Power Ball" lottery tickets. To ease the pressure, Congress also added 20,000 additional visas for aliens earning master's degrees at U.S. institutions. These scholars can apply for their work visas outside the normal application process. The Senate is expected to pass a bill in late 2006 that will raise the cap to 115,000 per year; whether the House of Representatives will go along is uncertain, given the climate of controversy. But if such a change takes place, it could also include extension of exemptions to the quota for science and math experts, also making getting their green cards subsequently simpler, too.

The laws reiterate the prevailing-wage rates and non-displacement protections of preceding legislation and give the U.S. Department of Labor new authority to investigate and enforce the rules against employers, allowing the Department of Labor to initiate such enforcement activities even in the absence of a U.S. worker complaint.

3. L-1 visas for "specialized knowledge" alien workers were also reformed by the new laws. L-1 workers entering the United States will no longer be eligible for lending out to third parties. And "blanket" L-1 visas, covering a whole cadre of foreign nationals, will be available only to groups of employees from foreign affiliates of the applying employer, and only if these workers have been employed as executives, managers, or specialists for a full year by the foreign affiliate.

With these relatively modest reforms in effect, the second year of President Bush's second administration opened with a passionate battle over immigration reform both in Congress and in the streets. The highly conservative House passed a bill intended to make illegal-immigrant status a felony. The less-strident Senate passed its own measure, reflecting the President's notion of guest-worker status for illegal aliens who step forward, pay fines, learn English, and begin the march toward U.S. citizenship. As the two houses wrestled over which, if any, measure might be sent down Pennsylvania Avenue to the Oval Office, immigrant advocacy groups hit the bricks in Washington and in other major metropolitan centers around the nation. When waving Mexican flags met with condemnation, many protesters switched to Old Glory, emphasizing the alleged affection of illegal immigrants for American soil.

In sum, U.S. immigration policies remain a source of political controversy and conflict. As this Supplement went to press it was impossible to predict what the outcome might be. Consequently, the authors have devoted a portion of this chapter to providing a compilation of the various sources of guidance that employers, managers, and attorneys can conveniently consult for assistance in navigating these boiling waters.

Basics

Q 12:3   Where can these laws be accessed?

These federal laws can be accessed on the website for the new U.S. Citizenship and Immigration Services (USCIS), which is one of the two successors to the former Immigration and Naturalization Service (INS). The website is http://uscis.gov/graphics/lawsregs/amendina.htm.

Federal Government Information and Guidance

1. U.S. Citizenship and Immigration Services.

   On March 1, 2003, service and benefit functions of the U.S. Immigration and Naturalization Service (INS) transitioned into the Department of Homeland Security (DHS) as the U.S. Citizenship and Immigration Services (USCIS). The President nominated Eduardo Aguirre to lead the USCIS; he was confirmed by the Senate on June 19, 2003. The USCIS is responsible for the administration of immigration and naturalization adjudication functions and establishing immigration services policies and priorities. These functions include:

   - adjudication of immigrant visa petitions;
   - adjudication of naturalization petitions;
   - adjudication of asylum and refugee applications;
   - adjudications performed at the service centers, and
   - all other adjudications performed by the INS.

   [http://www.uscis.gov/graphics/aboutus/index.htm]

2. U.S. Immigration and Customs Enforcement.

   Created in March 2003, Immigration and Customs Enforcement (ICE) is the largest investigative branch of the Department of Homeland Security (DHS). The agency was created after [September 11, 2001] by combining the law enforcement arms of the former [INS] and the former U.S. Customs Service, to more effectively enforce our immigration and customs laws so as to protect the United States against terrorist attacks. ICE does this by targeting illegal immigrants: the people, money, and materials that support terrorism and other criminal activities. ICE is a key component of the DHS "layered defense" approach to protecting the nation.

   [http://www.ice.gov/about/index.htm]

3. U.S. Department of Justice. The DOJ mission statement provides this list of responsibilities: "to enforce the law and defend the interests of the United States according to the law; to ensure public safety against threats foreign and domestic; to provide federal leadership in preventing and controlling crime; to seek just punishment for those guilty of unlawful behavior; and to ensure fair and impartial administration of justice for all Americans."

   [http://www.usdoj.gov/02organizations/]

   The Office of Special Counsel for Immigration-Related Unfair Employment Practices (OSC), in the Civil Rights Division, is responsible for enforcing the antidiscrimination provisions of the Immigration and Nationality Act (INA), 8 U.S.C. § 1324b, which protect U.S. citizens and legal immigrants from employment discrimination based upon citizenship or immigration status and national origin, from unfair documentary practices relating to the employment eligibility verification process, and from retaliation.

[http://www.usdoj.gov/crt/osc/htm/WebOverview2005.htm]

4. U.S. Social Security Administration.

The Social Security Administration (SSA) is headquartered in Baltimore, Maryland and has 10 regional offices and 1,300 local offices nationwide. [The agency] pays retirement, disability, and survivors benefits to workers and their families and administers the Supplemental Security Income program. [It] also issues Social Security numbers.

[http://www.ssa.gov/aboutus/]

"In general, only non-citizens who have permission to work from the DHS can apply for a Social Security number." [http://www.ssa.gov]

5. Federal Bureau of Investigation.

On September 4, 2001, Robert S. Mueller, III became the 6th Director of the Federal Bureau of Investigation. Since the tragic events of September 11, 2001, one week into his term, he became responsible for spearheading what is perhaps the most extensive reorganization the FBI has experienced since its conception. By May 2002, he articulated 10 top FBI priorities: protecting the United States from terrorist attacks, from foreign intelligence operations, and from cyber-based attacks and high-technology crimes; combating public corruption at all levels; protecting civil rights; combating international and national organized crime, major white-collar crime, and significant violent crime; supporting our law enforcement and intelligence partners; and upgrading FBI technology. "While we remain committed to our other important national security and law enforcement responsibilities, the prevention of terrorism takes precedence in our thinking and planning; in our hiring and staffing; in our training and technologies; and, most importantly, in our investigations," Director Mueller has said.

[http://www.fbi.gov/aboutus.htm]

6. U.S. Department of Labor.

The Department of Labor fosters and promotes the welfare of the job seekers, wage earners, and retirees of the United States by improving their working conditions, advancing their opportunities for profitable employment, protecting their retirement and health care benefits, helping employers find workers, strengthening free collective bargaining, and tracking changes in employment, prices, and other national economic measurements. In carrying out this mission, the Department administers a variety of Federal labor laws, including those that guarantee workers' rights to safe and healthful working conditions; a minimum hourly wage and overtime pay; freedom from employment discrimination; unemployment insurance; and other income support.

[http://www.dol.gov/opa/aboutdol/mission.htm]

The Immigration and Nationality Act (INA) sets forth the conditions for the temporary and permanent employment of aliens in the United States and includes provisions that address employment eligibility and employment verification. These provisions apply to all employers. DOL provides a wide variety of resources to aid employers with compliance.

[http://www.dol.gov/compliance/laws/comp-ina.htm]

7. U.S. Department of State. The State's mission statement reads as follows: "Create a more secure, democratic, and prosperous world for the benefit of the American people and the international community." [http://www.state.gov/s/d/rm/rls/dosstrat/2004/23503.htm] The Bureau of Consular Affairs within the State Department manages the visa process. Information on all types of visas can be found at http://travel.state.gov/visa/visa_1750.html.

Immigrant-Advocacy Organizations

1. Catholic Legal Immigration Network, Inc. This organization's mission is to enhance and expand delivery of legal services to indigent and low-income immigrants principally through diocesan immigration programs and to meet the immigration needs identified by the Catholic Church in the United States."

CLINIC fulfills its mission by:

- Providing a full range of legal and non-legal support services to 160-plus member agencies comprised of Catholic Charities and diocesan legal immigration programs. Member agencies serve poor immigrants seeking family reunification, citizenship, and protection from persecution and violence.

- Creating, funding and managing direct legal service projects that are national in scope and thus supplement local member agency capacity or expertise.

- Representing archdioceses, dioceses, and religious congregations that need foreign-born priests, nuns, and lay religious workers to serve immigrant communities in the United States.

[http://www.cliniclegal.org/Aboutus.html]

2. National Network for Immigrant and Refugee Rights.

The National Network for Immigrant and Refugee Rights (NNIRR) is a national organization composed of local coalitions and immigrant, refugee, community, religious, civil rights and labor organizations and activists. It serves as a forum to share information and analysis, to educate communities and the general public, and to develop and coordinate plans of action on important immigrant and refugee issues.

[http://www.nnirr.org/about/about_mission.html]

3. American Immigration Lawyers Association.

The American Immigration Lawyers Association (AILA) is the national association of over 9,500 attorneys and law professors who practice and teach immigration law. AILA Member attorneys represent tens of thousands of U.S. families who have applied for permanent residence for their spouses, children, and other close relatives to lawfully enter and reside in the United States. AILA members also represent thousands of U.S. businesses and industries who sponsor highly skilled foreign workers seeking to enter the United States in a temporary or—having proven the unavailability of U.S. workers—permanent basis. AILA members also represent foreign students, entertainers, athletes, and asylum seekers, often on a pro bono basis. Founded in 1946, AILA is a nonpartisan, nonprofit organization that provides its Members with continuing legal education, information, professional services, and expertise through its 35 chapters and over 50 national committees. AILA is an Affiliated Organization of the American Bar Association and is represented in the ABA House of Delegates.

[http://www.aila.org/content/default.aspx?docid=1021]

Other Immigration-Policy Organizations

1. Federation for American Immigration Reform.

The Federation for American Immigration Reform (FAIR) is a national, nonprofit, public-interest, membership organization of concerned citizens who share a common belief that our nation's immigration policies must be reformed to serve the national interest.

FAIR seeks to improve border security, to stop illegal immigration, and to promote immigration levels consistent with the national interest—more traditional rates of about 300,000 a year.

With more than 198,000 members and supporters nationwide, FAIR is a non-partisan group whose membership runs the gamut from liberal to conservative.

[http://www.fairus.org/site/PageServer?pagename=about_aboutmain]

2. American Immigration Network. The network provides U.S. "immigration services for individuals, businesses, and organizations by a team of experienced, licensed immigration attorneys." The organization's "popular kits are, in many cases, an inexpensive alternative to retaining an attorney. Each kit contains all the required forms, required supporting documents,

sample forms, sample letters, extremely easy to understand instructions, [USCIS and DOL] addresses and phone numbers, and much more."

[http://www.usavisanow.com/]

3. BNA Web Watch. The website provides links to government, industry, and academic resources on selected topics spanning the breadth of BNA coverage. New subjects are posted weekly, and new resources are also added to existing topics. Immigration reform issues are updated daily at http://www.bna.com/webwatch/immigrationreform.htm.

Q 12:21.1   What are the estimated costs connected with properly verifying the legality of immigrant workers?

One of the proposals afloat in the Congress for immigrant verification and control is an electronic employment-verification system aimed at screening approximately 54 million new hires annually. The Government Accountability Office estimates that creation, dissemination, and operation of this proposed system could cost $11.7 billion. Employer cost per employee is expected to run somewhere between $10 and $50. One thing seems certain: the seldom-enforced requirement of the Immigration Reform and Control Act of 1986 (passed the last time the United States granted amnesty to its illegal aliens), that employers verify the legitimacy of their workers, will no longer be winked at by the federal government, regardless of what other provisions a new immigration statute may contain.

Discrimination Against Aliens

Q 12:61.1   Are the children of illegal immigrants entitled to attend public schools?

Yes. As early as 1982, the U.S. Supreme Court held that:

- Illegal aliens are included under the protections provided by the equal protection clause of the 14th Amendment to the U.S. Constitution.
- The discrimination inherent in a Texas statute, which withheld state education funding from school districts for illegal immigrants, and which allowed school districts to deny enrollment to such "illegals," was not "rational," unless it furthered a substantial state goal.
- The "illegal" status of the children in question, standing alone, was an insubstantial reason for denying them the same educational opportunities as other children in their communities.
- No national policy exists for denying such children an elementary education.
- The state's rationale—preservation of finite funding—was insufficient to sustain the statute against constitutional challenge.

[Plyler v. Doe, 457 U.S. 202 (U.S. 1982)]

Q 12:61.2 Has the Supreme Court said that aliens are entitled to pay reduced in-state tuition to attend state universities?

Yes. In *Toll v. Moreno* [458 U.S. 1 (U.S. 1982)], the Supreme Court declared that a Maryland statute, which denied certain aliens the opportunity to pay the reduced rate at the University of Maryland, violated the supremacy clause of the Constitution.

Q 12:61.3 Has Congress enacted any laws in response to the Supreme Court's decisions regarding aliens' rights to enjoy the same educational benefits as states afford their own citizens?

Yes, two statutes enacted within weeks of one another in 1996 are widely viewed as being, among other things, responses to the Supreme Court's 1982 rulings, which afforded the children of illegal aliens the right to attend public schools and required states to provide alien residents the same reduced in-state tuition rates available to resident citizens. These two statutes are:

1. The Personal Responsibility and Work Opportunity Reconciliation Act of 1996 (PRWORA) [H.R. 3734], and

2. The Illegal Immigration Reform and Immigrant Responsibility Act of 1996 (IIRIRA) [Pub. L. No. 104–208].

Q 12:61.4 What does the IIRIRA say about aliens' access to state-sponsored benefits?

The IIRIRA contains the following relevant provisions:

1. In general, illegal aliens are "not eligible for any State or local public benefit."

2. Exceptions to the general rule are made for (a) emergency medical care; (b) short-term, in-kind emergency disaster relief; (c) public health immunization and treatment of the symptoms of communicable diseases; (d) soup kitchens and similar fundamental services for the protection of life and safety.

3. "State or local public benefit" is defined as "any grant, contract, loan, professional license, or commercial license provided by an agency of a State or local government" or by their appropriated funds.

[8 U.S.C. § 1621]

Q 12:61.5 Do any states allow illegal immigrants to attend their public universities at reduced, in-state tuition rates?

Yes, currently the following states have statutes permitting illegal aliens to attend their public universities at the reduced, in-state tuition rates:

1. California

2. Illinois

3. Kansas

4. New York

5. Oklahoma

6. Texas

7. Utah

8. Washington

By contrast, two states, Alaska and Mississippi, have statutes that specifically prevent illegal aliens from attending their higher education institutions at reduced, in-state rates.

Q 12:61.6   Have state statutes that allow illegal aliens to attend public universities at reduced, in-state tuition rates been challenged?

Yes. In 2004, a group of non-resident students filed suit in federal court challenging a Kansas statute [Kan. Stat. Ann. § 76–731a] that had taken effect on July 1, 2004, and that allowed undocumented aliens to attend Kansas state universities and to pay in-state rates. The plaintiffs challenged the state statute on the basis of:

1. The 1996 Illegal Immigration Reform and Immigrant Responsibility Act (see Qs 12:61.3 and 12:61.4);

2. The equal protection clause of the Fourteenth Amendment of the U.S. Constitution; and

3. Federal preemption principles, notably the Student and Exchange Visitor Information System (SEVIS).

The U.S. District Court for Kansas dismissed the plaintiffs' action without ruling on its substantive claims, holding that they lacked standing to sue. The district judge reasoned that issuing an injunction against the state officials/defendants would deny illegal aliens the reduced tuition rate without benefiting the plaintiffs in any direct way. Furthermore, said the judge, the 1996 statute does not create any private right of action. [Day v. Sebelius, 376 F. Supp. 2d 1022 (D. Kan. 2005)]

In December 2005 another group of plaintiffs commenced a similar action against the regents of the University of California system, likewise challenging a statute that enables illegal aliens resident in the state to pay reduced tuition rates, while the plaintiffs and similarly situated, out-of-state students pay greater, often substantially greater, tuition bills. While opponents of the plaintiffs are predicting an outcome similar to the Kansas case, a difference here is that the plaintiffs are seeking hundreds of millions of dollars in damages for their class, claiming not that the "illegals" must be denied the lower rate, but rather that they themselves are entitled to the same benefit under the equal protection clause and the federal immigration acts.

Immigration Act of 1990

Q 12:62   What is the *Immigration Act of 1990*?

Primarily, the *Immigration Act of 1990* constituted a restructuring of this nation's priorities in admitting skilled immigrants. This landmark legislation increased the annual maximum of employment-based visas from 54,000 to 140,000. Also, the Act replaced the 20,000-visas-per-country standard with new calculations that were intended to benefit citizens from countries considered by Congress to have been affected adversely by prior legislation. Additionally, total family-based visas were annually increased to 465,000 for each of the next three federal Fiscal Years, then to 480,000 thereafter.

Q 12:63   What categories of skilled immigrants did the Immigration Act of 1990 favor?

The law authorized the annual increase in permanent resident visas from 54,000 to 140,000 in five categories:

1. *Priority workers.* These are defined as immigrants with "extraordinary ability" in the arts, athletics, business, education, or the sciences. The application must reflect a national or international reputation, extensively documented achievements, and the stated intention to continue working in the field of high accomplishment plus the potential to "substantially benefit" the United States. Also included in this category are internationally recognized professors with substantial teaching or research experience, plus an offer of tenure or a tenure-track position at a U.S. institution. Executives sponsored and employed by multinational corporations are also included.

2. *Professionals with advanced degrees and aliens of exceptional ability.* In lieu of the "extraordinary ability" required of priority workers, "exceptional ability" plus labor certification, such as a job offer, is required. A bachelor's degree plus five years of experience is likely to be the bare minimum to meet this category's alternative criterion of an advanced degree.

3. *Other professionals and skilled workers.* Along with having labor certification, applicants must offer some special skill or a bachelor's degree.

4. *Special immigrants.* This category includes, for example, ministers and other religious workers.

5. *Investors.* The category consists of immigrants willing and able to invest at least $1 million in a business that will employ at least 10 Americans. The requisite investment can be more modest for as many as 3,000 of these applicants who intend to put their money in certain targeted areas, such as rural regions or locales with high unemployment.

Q 12:64   What does the Immigration Act of 1990 require with regard to family-based immigration quotas?

The Act increases the number of available visas overall and, in particular, it increases visas allotted to the spouses and minor children of permanent resident aliens in the following preferential order:

1. Unmarried sons and daughters of U.S. citizens;
2. Spouses, minor children, and unmarried sons and daughters (regardless of age) of permanent resident aliens;
3. Married sons and daughters of U.S. citizens; and
4. Sisters and brothers of adult U.S. citizens.

Q 12:65   Are there any regulations interpreting and enforcing the Immigration Act of 1990?

Yes. The regulations are published at 8 C.F.R. Parts 1, 103, 214, 274a, and 299; 22 C.F.R. Part 44; 24 C.F.R. Part 49; and 29 C.F.R. Part 501.

Q 12:69   Does the Immigration Act of 1990 provide any protection against displacement of U.S. employees by immigrants?

The law requires the Department of Labor (DOL) to balance its increases in employment-based immigration with specific new protections for U.S. citizens. These protections include employer notification to employees in advance of hiring aliens. Such an employer will have to notify either the affected employees' union or post notices in the plant if the employees are not organized. A second protection mandated by the new law is "attestation-like processes" to protect the wages and working conditions of Americans when companies hire certain categories of nonimmigrant aliens, such as D-Visa crews to perform longshoremen's work, H-1B specialty occupations, and students with F-visas who accept off-campus employment. Employers hiring such temporary employees must file attestations with the DOL to the effect that they will pay prevailing wages and provide appropriate working conditions. Employees will have a grievance procedure through which to challenge these hiring practices.

A third mandate requires the DOL to develop a labor market information program to identify occupational shortages and surpluses of skilled workers for streamlining visa processing while hopefully protecting Americans who might otherwise be displaced from overstocked occupations.

The law also calls for state grants to be used to educate and train U.S. workers to fill shortage categories that would otherwise be filled by alien employees. Underemployed Americans are to be the special targets for these grants.

Q 12:70 Where can I find compliance information regarding the Immigration Act of 1990?

See the DOL website at http://www.dol.gov/dol/compliance/comp-ina.htm. This site offers links to all relevant regulations, including the following:

1. The law;

2. The regulations;

3. Regulations on the Temporary Employment of Aliens in the United States; and

4. Regulations on Enforcement of Contractual Obligations for Temporary Alien/Agricultural Workers Admitted under Section 216 of the INA.

DOL Guidance Materials:

1. Employment Law Guide: Authorized Workers

2. Employment Law Guide: Crewmembers (D-1 Visas)

3. Employment Law Guide: Workers in Professional and Specialty Occupations (H-1B Visas)

4. H-1B (Professional and Specialty Occupation Visas) Interim Final Regulations Fact Sheet

5. Employment Law Guide: Nurses (H-1C Visas)

6. Employment Law Guide: Temporary Agricultural Workers (H-2A Visas)

7. H-2A (Temporary Agricultural Worker Visas) Fact Sheet

8. Employment Law Guide: Temporary Nonagricultural Workers (H-2B Visas)

9. Employment Law Guide: Permanent Employment of Workers Based on Immigration

Forms and Instructions:

1. Foreign Labor Certification (Employment & Training Administration)

2. Form I-9, Employment Eligibility Verification

3. Application of U.S. Labor Laws to Immigrant Workers Fact Sheet

4. Application of U.S. Labor Laws to Immigrant Worker Fact Sheet (Korean) (PDF)

5. Aplicación de las Leyes Laborales de los EE UU a Obreros Inmigrantes Hoja de Datos (Español)

6. Fair Labor Standards Act Application to Foreign Commercial Vehicle Operators Fact Sheet

7. Aplicación de la Ley de Normas Razonables de Trabajo a los Conductores Extranjeros de Vehículos Comerciales Hoja de Datos (Español)

Q 12:76 What are the most important things to know about an H-1B visa?

1. The H-1B is the most common temporary-worker visa. It is initially issued for a three-year period and is subject to renewal for an additional

three years. [*See* 8 C.F.R. § 215.2(h) and Public Law 107-273, American Competitiveness in the Twenty-First Century Act of 2002]

2. In limited circumstances the H-1B may extended in one-year increments beyond the usual six-year limit.

3. Processing an H-1B typically takes three to five months. However, premium processing (15 days) is available for an additional $1,000 fee, payable to CIS.

4. Transfer of H-1B status from one employer to another is permitted if: (a) the alien entered the U.S. lawfully; (b) the alien has not violated her or his status by working in the U.S. without authorization; and (c) the transfer request is filed before the expiration of the alien's current H-1B status. This is called "H-1B portability" and is done via a portability petition. The employee may work for the new employer while the position is pending; however, if the portability petition is denied, employment authorization ends immediately.

5. Prior to filing an H-1B petition, the employer must obtain an approved Form ETA-9035, Labor Condition Application (LCA). This is obtained from the DOL, which will issue it if the employer attests that it will: (a) pay the alien worker the higher of the prevailing wage for the occupation or the wage paid to U.S. workers performing the same job; and (b) hiring the alien will not adversely affect wages and working conditions of U.S. workers. The application has been streamlined and can be electronically filed on the DOL website.

6. The employer also must post notices of the job opening at two locations on the work site for 10 working days before filling the position with the alien worker. Note that the position need not be otherwise advertised to U.S. workers.

7. Employers must maintain a "public access file" for each of their H-1B employees. The file should be created within 24 hours of filing the Labor Condition Application with the DOL. This file must contain: proof of the prevailing wage; a copy of the LCA; verification of job posting; proof that the alien employee received a copy of the LCA; statement of the wage rate; an actual wage statement; and benefits documentation. The file must be maintained for at least a year beyond the length of employment.

Relationship of Other Laws to Aliens and Immigration

Q 12:130   What types of non-immigrant student visas does the USCIS issue?

The USCIS issues three general types of non-immigrant student visas:

1. The F-1 visa is issued to international (alien) students who typically intend to study in the United States for several years and earn a degree.

2. The J-1 visa is issued to international students who are exchange visitors to the United States, studying at an American university for a semester

or two and then returning to their home institutions to complete their studies.

3. The M-1 visa is similar to the F-1 but is issued to international students studying at post-secondary trade schools.

Q 12:131 How are international students tracked by the U.S. Immigration Control and Enforcement (ICE) agency?

All post-secondary schools that admit international students must track these students on the Student and Exchange Visitor Information System (SEVIS), a computer database accessible only to designated school officials and responsible officers.

Q 12:132 Are international students holding F-1 visas allowed to work?

The answer is a qualified, and complicated, "yes." Some of the main circumstances under which such students may work are:

- They may work on campus at the institutions they are attending, provided they have Social Security numbers.

- After one academic year, F-1 students are allowed to apply for Optional Practical Training (OPT). OPT is available on a full- or part-time basis with third parties, including private corporations, provided the job relates to the course of study pursued by the student. Students typically reserve their period of OPT eligibility (one year full-time or two years part-time) for after graduation.

- F-1 students also may work for third parties off campus if they can establish an economic hardship that did not exist at the time that they were issued visas to attend school in the United States.

- After one academic year of university attendance in the United States, an F-1 student may be permitted to work for a third-party employer off campus under a university-sponsored program of Curricular Practical Training (CPT). Typically, a bona fide CPT program must be for college credit and be an integral part of the student's curricular requirements. Use of CPT typically does not prevent subsequent use of OPT.

Q 12:133 How does an F-1 visa holder go about getting a Social Security number?

The Social Security Administration requires that an F-1 visa holder applying for a Social Security number present the following four documents:

1. A valid passport;

2. A valid INS Form I-20, issued by the university he or she is attending;

3. A valid F-1 visa; and

4. An offer letter from the prospective employer (which usually will be the university the student is attending).

The Administration is then required to provide the local office or sub-office of the U.S. ICE agency an opportunity to review and approve the application. This requirement sometimes can result in a lengthy delay in the issuance of the Social Security number, although most applications are successfully processed within a couple of weeks. Delays can sometimes be overcome by employer recourse to the office of the local congressional representative, which typically has a staffer charged with assisting constituents in such matters.

Q 12:134   Can international students employed under one-year OPT authorizations become permanent employees of the company?

Yes. Most international students seeking OPT employment opportunities with American corporations have hopes of remaining in the United States and in the employ of these American companies. The one-year OPT commitment enables the employer to ascertain the alien worker's suitability for long-term employment with the firm. In instances where the relationship has proved promising, the company's human resources department can sponsor the alien worker for an H-1B visa. The H-1B visa, if obtained, is good for three years with the possibility of a single renewal period of like length. From there, the alien-employee typically will apply for permanent residency (i.e., a "green card").

Q 12:135   Are J-1 exchange students allowed to work while studying in the United States?

Like their F-1 counterparts (see Q 12.132), J-1 exchange students are allowed to work on campus if they have Social Security numbers. In order to obtain a Social Security number, a J-1 exchange student must apply at a local Social Security Administration office and present with his or her application the following four documents:

1. A valid passport;
2. A valid J-1 visa;
3. A valid DS (Department of State) Form 2019; and
4. A letter from the university's responsible office allowing employment.

J-1 exchange students also are allowed to work for third-party employers off campus for purposes of practical training, if the program is approved by the responsible officer. Such employment for training purposes can occur during or immediately after the studies pursued on the college campus.

Q 12:136   How does an F-1 international student qualify for OPT?

International students holding F-1 visas must meet the following requirements to qualify for OPT:

- The student can apply no sooner than one academic year after commencing his or her U.S. studies.

- The student must apply before completing those studies.
- The application is sent to the USCIS service center with jurisdiction over the university where the student is studying.
- The applicant need not have a specific job offer in hand at the time of application, but must express intent to pursue a job opportunity related to his or her course of study.
- The applicant must have maintained unbroken F-1 status while in the United States and must hold a valid passport and INS Form I-20.

Q 12:137   What is an M-1 visa?

The M-1 category includes students in vocational or other nonacademic programs, other than language training. Approval for the attendance of nonacademic students may be solicited by a community college or junior college that provides vocational or technical training and awards associate degrees; a vocational high school; a trade school; or a school of nonacademic training other than language training. Employment rules under this category are approximately the same as under the F-1 visa (see Q 12:136).

The Immigration Act of 2006

Q 12:138   What is the status of the proposed Immigration Act of 2006?

As this 2007 Supplement goes to press, the Senate has voted 62 to 36 to approve compromise immigration reform legislation (S. 2611, the Comprehensive Immigration Reform Act of 2006), thus setting the stage for what appears likely to be a contentious House-Senate conference, in which the Senate-passed bill would have to be harmonized with the harsh, enforcement-only bill (H.R. 4437) passed by the House in December 2005. Despite attempts by a handful of senators to fundamentally alter the bill that was reported out of the Senate Judiciary Committee in March 2006, the basic architecture of comprehensive immigration reform survived essentially intact after nearly four weeks of senate floor debate on the measure and votes on more than 40 proposed amendments.

Q 12:139   What are the highlights of the comprehensive Senate bill?

The main features of the Senate's comprehensive legislation include:

- A path to permanent legal status for most of the estimated 12 million undocumented immigrants in the United States,
- A new temporary worker program,
- Significant increases in family- and employment-based permanent visas (green cards),
- Reforms to the agricultural worker program,
- Reforms to the "high-skill" immigration programs,

- Assistance for undocumented high school graduates in achieving college educations (the DREAM Act), and

- Some very harsh enforcement provisions (echoing the House bill).

Q 12:140 What were some of the reactions to the prospect of passage of an Immigration Act of 2006 after the passage of the Senate-approved bill?

Following passage of a comprehensive reform bill by the Senate in late May 2006, reactions spanned the spectrum of political positions on immigration reform. The following sample comments represent the pro-immigration and anti-immigration camps in the debate.

- The president of the American Immigration Lawyers Association (AILA), Deborah Notkin, stated, "This historic action by the Senate creates the possibility that our 20th century immigration laws may finally be reformed to meet the needs of a 21st century America." A copy of the full comment can be found at www.aila.org/content/default.aspx?docid=19508.

- The Federation for American Immigration Reform (FAIR) predicted, "The approved bill would send the U.S. population skyrocketing towards a billion people by the close of the century—with no analysis done of the impacts of this mass population explosion on housing, congestion, overcrowding, education, the environment and the overall quality of life." The full statement can be found at www.fairus.org/site/PageServer?pagename=media_release5252006.

Chapter 13

Employment Termination

Employment termination is far and away the most likely source of employment litigation. No single action or procedure can prevent all wrongful discharge suits and employment discrimination charges, but the human resources professional or company executive who recognizes where the dangers lie can vastly increase the odds of preventing litigation or reducing exposure if litigation is filed. This chapter discusses recent cases addressing various issues involving the federal Worker Adjustment and Retraining Notification Act (WARN).

Plant Closings, Mass Layoffs, and WARN

Q 13:38   When does the exception for unforeseeable business circumstances apply?

Business circumstances that were not reasonably foreseeable when the 60-day notice would have had to have been sent excuse the employer in the case of plant closings and mass layoffs. An important indication of a business circumstance that is not reasonably foreseeable is a sudden, dramatic, and unexpected action or condition outside the employer's control. For example, a strike at the employer's major supplier, an important client's unexpected withdrawal from a major contract with the employer, an unexpected and severe economic downturn, and a government-ordered closing of an employment site without prior notice might be considered business circumstances that could not have been foreseen.

In *Roquet v. Arthur Andersen LLP* [398 F.3d 585 (7th Cir. 2005)], a class of former employees brought a WARN Act claim against Arthur Andersen for its failure to provide 60 days notice prior to laying them off in connection with Arthur Andersen's much publicized break-up in 2002. Arthur Andersen defended by saying that its need to lay off employees was sudden and dramatic and a result of the Department of Justice's (DOJ's) announcement on March 1, 2002, that it was going to seek an indictment against the company. The court, after reviewing the facts and the disastrous consequences this news had on its business, concluded that the mass layoffs and terminations that were determined to be necessary soon after the DOJ's notice clearly fell within the unforeseen business circumstances exception. As the court concluded, the reason for layoffs was not reasonably foreseeable 60 days before the decision to lay off employees was made. Although Arthur Andersen had known for some time it was under investigation, the news of the indictment was "sudden, dramatic and unexpected," with disastrous impact on the business such that no violation of WARN was found.

Q 13:40.1   Can lenders of companies who are in control of financial decisions be liable for back pay and benefits upon a finding of a WARN Act violation?

A few courts in recent years have been asked to determine whether liability for WARN violations can extend beyond the employer to lenders and secured creditors who are said to be in control of the employer's financial decisions during periods of delinquency. This issue arises because the WARN Act applies to mass plant closings and layoffs, many of which are defunct companies, and it is not unusual for creditors to become intimately involved with companies in trying to save their investment before the bottom falls out. Because the defunct companies may not have the wherewithal to pay for violations, plaintiffs are attempting to determine whether this liability can be extended to the company's lenders, who obviously are in a better position to pay any penalties. In *Smith v. Ajax Magnathermic Corp.* [144 Fed. Appx. 482 (6th Cir. 2005)], the plaintiff was attempting to hold a consortium of lenders liable for WARN Act violations, alleging that the consortium of lenders was in actual control of the business operations and had inserted a consulting firm to manage the employer's operations on a day-to-day basis. Although the court noted that previous cases had failed because the lender defendants typically do not have sufficient control over the operations to be held liable, nonetheless, it adopted the Ninth Circuit's analysis that if sufficient control of the business enterprise in a normal commercial sense can be demonstrated, lender liability under WARN may be appropriate. However, if the degree of control is no more than the creditor's seeking to protect its security interests and acting only to preserve the business assets for liquidation or sale, liability under WARN would not come into play. Because the plaintiff in *Smith* had alleged sufficient facts to establish the level of control required to maintain a claim under WARN against the lenders, the court reversed the dismissal of the WARN Act claim against the lenders and remanded the matter for further proceedings.

Chapter 14

Managing Labor and Employment Litigation

The corporation that has not experienced some form of employment litigation is the exception. Despite all the advice that an employer gleans from attorneys, accountants, and other outside advisers—and despite all the best intentions of management—lawsuits and charges still occur. This chapter discusses the litigation process and provides practical advice on avoiding employee claims, managing cases, and controlling litigation costs and expenses.

Avoiding Employee Claims

Q 14:25   What can employers do to help reduce their risk of exposure to employee claims?

Although there is no magic wand that can eliminate claims, reasonable procedures adopted by employers can minimize the risk of being sued and, if they are sued, reduce the exposure. Below is a set of guidelines geared toward this goal:

- *The hiring process.* There are numerous protected categories under both federal and state civil rights laws. Interviewers should be admonished not to treat applicants differently on the basis of protective categories, or make any inquiry into protected areas, lest the applicant think that such inquiry is an indication of bias. As to issues of disability, it is always advisable that no inquiry as to a medical condition be made, even if apparent and obvious, until after a bona fide offer of employment.

- *Harassment.* Employers should adopt and disseminate a written policy against harassment in all forms. The policy should both encourage complaints and provide for a prompt and thorough investigation of complaints. Employees and supervisors should be trained to identify illegal harassment, know their responsibilities for coming forward to complain of harassment, and be familiar with the investigation process.

- *Civil rights training.* Employees and supervisors should to be trained as to how discrimination claims can be maintained, both through direct evidence and circumstantial evidence, together with additional emphasis on retaliation and public policy claims.

- *Written discipline.* Supervisors need to mete out written discipline when needed and take the time to provide accurate performance evaluations.

- *Discharge of an employee.* Before discharging an employee, an employer should review the matter to ensure that a proper investigation for the infraction has been taken, that the discipline is even-handed and consistent with the individual's personnel file, and that similar infractions for similarly situated employees resulted in similar discipline. If the discharge is for poor performance over time, there should be prior written discipline alerting the employee of the problem and notifying the employee that his or her job is in jeopardy if poor performance continues.

- *Avoid bad timing.* Bad timing issues come into play in a number of different types of lawsuits, including pregnancy discrimination claims, retaliation claims, and whistleblower claims. If an employee suffers an adverse employment action soon after the employee declares her pregnancy, complains of harassment, or threatens to report the employer to a government agency, the tendency is to believe that the action was taken for an improper or illegal motive, absent clear proof to the contrary.

- *Family and Medical Leave Act (FMLA).* Supervisors should understand the employer's FMLA policies and procedures and be trained to spot time off that may be allocable to an employee's FMLA allotment.

Q 14:26 What is a *labor audit?*

The term *labor audit* refers to a process of review and analysis typically undertaken by an employment lawyer to determine what, if any, recommendations should be made to help reduce an employer's risk and exposure to employee claims.

Although there are no formal guidelines for this process, it generally includes the following:

- Review of applications and the hiring process and procedures;
- Review of mandatory postings;
- Review of disciplinary forms and procedures;
- Review of handbook or other written policies and procedures;

- Consideration of necessary training of employees and/or supervisors; and
- Review of employee contracts such as non-competition agreements, confidentiality agreements, and/or assignment of invention agreements.

After a review has taken place, recommendations are typically made as to what the employer can do to create and/or modify its policies and procedures towards reducing the employer's risk and exposure to employment claims.

Chapter 15

Employment Law in the Global Marketplace

Americans do business in almost all of the approximately 200 sovereign nations of the world. The economies of these many countries span the spectrum from free markets to communist dictatorships (although these latter entities certainly have declined in number and influence over the past decade and a half). Political systems and governmental attitudes toward unions and workers' rights vary just as widely around the world. Labor and tax laws and practices necessarily vary just as dramatically.

Beyond these "business as usual" challenges of operating in a global marketplace, the events of the first few years of the 21st century have presented new, often unique challenges to America's multinational corporations and their employees around the world. The Sixth Edition and this 2007 Supplement are replete with timely information specific to these challenges. Our chapters on government contractors (chapter 9), public employees (chapter 10), and immigration issues (chapter 12) all contain up-to-date information arising out of and relating to America's "War on Terror." Chapter 7 ("Job Safety") is particularly pertinent to multinational employers.

As this chapter was being prepared, the United States remained embroiled in Iraq. Even though the transfer of sovereignty to an Iraqi regime was accomplished on June 30, 2004, a coalition government eluded the elected officials as spring 2006 slipped into summer. The victory of Hamas in Palestinian elections placed the United States in a quandary, as America continued to espouse democracy for the Middle East while refusing to deal with a regime that it still considers essentially a terrorist organization. Israel's July incursion into Lebanon expanded the conflict.

Meanwhile, manufacturing jobs, and even some service roles, continued their race around the globe in search of the lowest wage rates and most business-friendly public policies. For example, as the North American Free Trade Agreement (NAFTA) marked its 10th anniversary in 2004, economists confirmed that manufacturing jobs had fled, as predicted, south of our border by the hundreds of thousands. What was not so well predicted or expected was the trans-Pacific migration of many of these same jobs to the People's Republic of China, and from there on to South and Southeast Asia, where labor costs are even lower than in China and Mexico.

Even more surprising, perhaps, is the movement of service-sector work to foreign venues. This trend might be traced to American banks and credit-card companies establishing large paper-work "plants" in Ireland in the 1990s. India became the next big player, as Indian software developers educated in the United States actually began a reverse-migration movement back to the South Asian subcontinent. By 2004, Indian law schools had begun teaching American constitutional, statutory, and common law, as international law firms headquartered in the United States began sending their paralegal chores to Indian professionals. Midway through the first decade of this new century, multinational corporations and other American firms doing business abroad do indeed face new opportunities, challenges, and threats in the realm of human resources.

If the United States has found globalization a difficult phenomenon with which to cope, the members of the European Union have found the challenge even more troubling. As Muslim residents of France rioted for more economic opportunities and civil rights, the government attempted to enact a two-year trial period of employment for younger workers. This brought unions and students into the streets with the result that, as this Supplement went to press, the French president had tentatively acquiesced in the repeal of the provision. However, if the French regime backs away from this revision of the usual European rule of lifelong employment, this will do nothing to take the pressure off the European Union and its member states to find ways to become more efficient and competitive in the world markets. A victory for the labor-student coalition will be—in the authors' view—short lived.

International Labor Relations

Q 15:3.1   What role does the concept of corporate social responsibility play in the global marketplace?

According to Senior Fellow and Director of Globalization Studies Susan Aaronson of the Kenan Institute, Washington Center, global corporate social responsibility is:

- a foreign policy issue in that corporations are ambassadors of their nation's values;
- an economic issue in that America's future markets are overseas;
- a moral issue on which the reputation of the corporation, its management, and shareholders depends on doing business abroad.

Whether corporate social responsibility extends to treatment of foreign employees may depend upon the policies and laws of the host nation. For example, in a vigorous effort to eradicate child labor and slavery, Brazil has enacted a "National Pact" which includes placing firms profiting from child and slave workers on a so-called "Dirty List."

In the United Kingdom, a nation characterized in the recent past by protection and encouragement of labor (see Q 15:10), a Minister of Corporate Social Responsibility was appointed for the first time in 2000. The United Kingdom, Germany, and Belgium require private pension funds to report on the social responsibility performances of the companies in which they have invested their members' contributions. Because of their historically protective attitudes toward their labor forces, it must be noted that private pensions constitute only small fractions of the overall retirement schemes in these nations. Since 2001, the Dutch government has required all firms seeking taxpayer-funded export credits to attest to their adherence to specified social responsibility guidelines. In 2002, France for the first time mandated disclosure of corporate social and environmental performance.

Q 15:3.2   What are the characteristics of a socially responsible corporation in the global marketplace?

Unilever is frequently cited as an exemplar of corporate social responsibility. The firm's own vision statement is: "As a multi-local multinational we aim to play our part in addressing global environmental and social concerns through local actions and in partnership with local governments and organizations." [www.unilever.com/ourvalues/] It expands upon that vision statement in its corporate history, saying:

> In the late 19th century the businesses that would later become Unilever were among the most philanthropic of their time. They set up projects to improve the lot of their workers and created products with a positive social impact, making hygiene and personal care commonplace and improving nutrition through adding vitamins to foods that were already

daily staples. Today, Unilever still believes that success means acting with "the highest standards of corporate behavior towards our employees, consumers and the societies and world in which we live." Over the years we've launched or participated in an ever-growing range of initiatives to source sustainable supplies of raw materials, protect environments, support local communities and much more.

Through this timeline you'll see how our brand portfolio has evolved. At the beginning of the 21st century, our Path to Growth strategy focused us on global high-potential brands and our Vitality mission is taking us into a new phase of development. More than ever, our brands are helping people "feel good, look good and get more out of life"—a sentiment close to Lord Leverhulme's heart over a hundred years ago.

[www.unilever.com/ourcompany/aboutunilever/history/default.asp]

Now one of the largest global corporations, Unilever's published policy on employees is as follows:

Unilever is committed to diversity in a working environment where there is mutual trust and respect and where everyone feels responsible for the performance and reputation of our company. We will recruit, employ and promote employees on the sole basis of the qualifications and abilities needed for the work to be performed. We are committed to safe and healthy working conditions for all employees. We will not use any form of forced, compulsory or child labor. We are committed to working with employees to develop and enhance each individual's skills and capabilities. We respect the dignity of the individual and the right of employees to freedom of association. We will maintain good communications with employees through company based information and consultation procedures.

[www.unilever.com/ourvalues/purposeandprinciples/ourprinciples/]

These values are far from alien to U.S. society and corporations. The difference is that Unilever, a company with its genesis in the Lever Brothers firm of the 1890s, has reportedly put these policies into action in the global labor arena.

Q 15:12.1   Are any notable changes undermining the tenets of European corporatism?

The most noteworthy events of the past year have occurred in France, where new employment laws permit employers to impose a two-year trial period in hiring new employees who are younger than 26 years of age. The so-called "New Employment Contract" (*contrat nouvelle embauche* or CNE) law was enacted in August 2005. It permits employers with fewer than 20 workers to apply the two-year trial provision. The second statute, called the "First Employment Contract" (*contrat premiere enbauche* or CPE), expands the two-year trial period option to all employers, regardless of their workforce size. President Jacques Chirac signed this second measure on March 31, 2006.

Chirac's signing of the second statute set off widespread protests by unions and students. Even before the French president signed the measure, MSNBC reported a one-million-person protest spanning several major French cities. These protests were followed by a one-day national strike. The unions claimed that as many as three million people took part in rallies and protests. One such rally caused the closing of the Eiffel Tower to tourists. The immediate result, as this Supplement was being prepared, was a promise from the French government to sit down with the unions and discuss some of the statutes' more controversial provisions. Meanwhile, employers were being asked by government officials to hold off entering into CPE contracts until the modifications, if any, to the new law have been completed.

However, as this Supplement went to press, the key tenets of the CNE and CPE were as follows:

- The parties to an employment contract entered under the terms of the statutes may terminate the relationship with as little notice as two weeks to one month. The only procedural requirement is a registered letter. If the termination is discipline based, then the company's disciplinary rules must be followed.

- If the termination comes at the employer's initiative, a severance payment equal to 8 percent of the total compensation paid to the employee from date of hire to date of termination must be given. The employee also will be entitled to collect unemployment compensation benefits.

- The fired employee will be entitled to 20 hours of professional training at the employer's expense.

- After the initial two-year trial period, the standard rules governing indefinite-term employment contracts apply.

The laws' stated purpose was to address the French 10 percent unemployment rate by encouraging employers to hire more people. The CPE is expressly intended to encourage the hiring of more young workers by reducing the employer's risk of being stuck with an unsatisfactory worker long-term. Unemployment among the young is particularly acute, estimated at 21 percent nationally.

Note. As this Supplement went to press—and following days of labor and student protests—the French government indicated its willingness to repeal the two-year trial period law. Assuming repeal occurs, the effect of this backing-down upon anticipated future reform measures is uncertain but ominous.

Q 15:12.2   Do the new French statutes, permitting two-year trial periods for younger workers, comport with European Union employment policies?

EU Development Commissioner Louis Michel spoke up in favor of the new French statutes on March 27, 2006, saying that, "If France is not able to accept that the CPE (first employment contract) is a positive way of giving young people a chance, then I don't know what it would be able to reform one day."

This statement seemed to comport with the recommendations of a January 25, 2006, communication from the Commission of the European Communities to the

Spring 2006 European Council. The recommendations in the report included more research and development, with more efficiency and better coordination; working together on a European scale to ensure that research is translated into innovative products and services that feeds into growth and jobs; a market free of barriers and red tape, where rules are predictable and where dynamic companies can prosper; more people working in order to finance pensions and health care as populations get older; a lifecycle approach to work; and affordable childcare and a decent work-life balance.

The report included four action items to implement these broad goals:

1. Increasing investment in knowledge and innovation with the largest contribution to come from the private sector.

2. Unlocking of business potential, particularly by breaking down remaining barriers to easy access to internal markets.

3. Responding to globalization and aging, especially by putting more people to work and keeping them working longer.

4. Moving toward an efficient, integrated energy policy.

The third of these goals in particular seems to anticipate such national statutes as the French two-year trial period laws, enacted in late 2005 and early 2006 (see Q 15:12.1).

Q 15:17.1   Are Japanese corporations likely to be able to maintain the level of employee compensation and benefits historically afforded employees under rules of employment and collective bargaining agreements?

Some researchers have recently suggested that the Japanese situation prefigures what the United States can expect to face in another quarter century. Specifically, these investigators have focused on the following factors:

• The retirement burden faced by Japan today is where the United States is projected to be in 25 years.

• Japanese population growth at present is essentially flat.

• The elderly-dependency ratio—the number of people 65 and older divided by the size of the overall national population from 15 through 64—has risen in Japan from 9 percent to 28 percent from 1960 through 2003.

• The Japanese labor-force growth rate has plummeted to −1.32 percent annually.

[M. R. Randall & D. Y. Suk, "Demographic Divergence: Economic Weakness in Japan and Implications for the United States," *Current Research in Global Business*, V. 8, No. 12, Fall 2005, pp. 91–99]

Q 15:17.2   Have the Japanese found any solutions for their demographic dilemma?

According to knowledgeable investigators,

> There are several favorable findings from the recent experience of Japan. They appear to be coping relatively well with an aging population which the United States will not experience for many years. Their pension mechanisms are functioning, and their health care system is still performing well. Life expectancy among Japanese people at approximately 81 years in 2002 is among the highest in the world and it ranks well above life expectancy in the United States (approximately 77 years). At the same time, the share of GDP allocated to health care in Japan was 7.2% in 2002 compared to 12.8% for the United States.

[M. R. Randall & D. Y. Suk, "Demographic Divergence: Economic Weakness in Japan and Implications for the United States," *Current Research in Global Business*, V. 8, No. 12, Fall 2005, pp. 91–99]

This is a remarkable statement, given the demographics:

> Public policy, the media, and discussions with private citizens revealed a high level of concern for the implications of one in four persons in Japan being sixty-five or older. By 2025 the dependency ratio (the ratio of people under fifteen years plus those sixty-five and older to those aged fifteen to sixty-five, indicating in a general way the ratio of the dependent population to the working population) was expected to be two dependents for every three workers. The aging of the population was already becoming evident in the aging of the labor force and the shortage of young workers in the late 1980s, with potential impacts on employment practices, wages and benefits, and the roles of women in the labor force. The increasing proportion of elderly people in the population also had a major impact on government spending. As recently as the early 1970s, social expenditures amounted to only about 6% of Japan's national income. In 1992 that portion of the national budget was 18%, and it was expected that by 2025, 27% of national income would be spent on social welfare.

[http://en.wikipedia.org/wiki/Demographics_of_Japan]

The explanation lies in relatively recent reforms instituted by the government:

> In an attempt to improve the quality of elderly care, provide additional funding, and capitalize on efficiencies that have resulted from the intermixing of medical treatment and long-term care functions, the government implemented a long-term care insurance system in 2000. This system collects obligatory insurance contributions from a broad sector of the population (all persons aged 40 or older) and provides such services as home visits by home helpers, visits to care centers, and long-term stays in nursing homes for older persons suffering from senile dementia or confined to bed for health reasons. In each individual case, the need for such services has to be certified by city, town, or village offices in charge of administering the nursing care insurance system. Insurance contributions from persons aged 65 and older

("Type 1 insured persons") are collected by the local administrations in the form of deductions from these persons' pensions, while contributions from "Type 2 insured persons" between the ages of 40 and 64 are collected together with health insurance contributions as a lump sum. Beneficiaries of the system must be at least 40 years old and must pay, in addition to the regular insurance contributions, 10% of the cost of services received. Japan's nursing care insurance system is financed by: the national government (25%), prefectural and local governments (12.5% each), and insurance contributions (50%).

[http://web-jpn.org/factsheet/health/elderly.html]

International Organizations

Q 15:101.1   Are American labor unions using their global reach to organize U.S. corporations?

An organization called Union Network International announced at its August 2005 Chicago convention that signing global agreements with targeted companies will be that organization's focus going forward.

Q 15:101.2   What is Union Network International?

Union Network International (UNI) is an organization aimed at meeting the globalization of corporations, trade, and manufacturing head on. Reasoning that the global labor market no longer recognizes or is confined within the borders of traditional nation-states, UNI seeks to organize workers on an international scale. The organization targets multinational corporations, seeking to apply global pressure in order to organize local and regional corporate facilities. "When companies are local, unions can be local; when companies are national, unions must be national; when companies are global, unions must be global. Our aim is to build more effective alliances in multinationals," UNI explains. [www.union-network.org]

Q 15:101.3   Who belongs to UNI?

UNI claims to hold the allegiance of approximately 15 million workers in 900 unions in 150 countries, representing employees in the following economic sectors:

- Commerce
- Electricity
- Finance
- Gaming
- Graphical

- Hair & beauty
- IBITS (industry, business services, information and computer technology)
- Media, entertainment, and the arts
- Postal
- Property services (cleaning and security)
- Social insurance
- Telecom
- Tourism

[http://www.union-network.org/]

Q 15:101.4   On which employers has UNI focused?

UNI has targeted a list of 100 multinational employers. As this 2007 Supplement was being prepared, UNI had achieved labor contracts with the following targeted corporations:

- Carrefour (a Paris-based food retailer)
- Hennes & Mauritz of Sweden (trading as H&M stores in the United States)
- Falck (a Danish rescue, healthcare, and safety-training organization)
- Internet Security Systems (based in Atlanta, GA)
- Metro AG of Germany
- OTE (Greek telecommunications company)
- Telefónica (the Spanish telecom provider)

[http://www.union-network.org/UNIsite/In_Depth/Multinationals/Multinationals.html]

In total, according to UNIs General Secretary Philip Jennings, the organization now boasts 50 signed collective agreements and another 50 in various stages of negotiation.

Q 15:101.5   How can UNI be contacted?

UNI's contact information is as follows:

Union Network International

8–10 Avenue Reverdil

CH-1260 Nyon

Tel. +41 22 365 21 00

Fax: +41 22 365 21 21

E-mail: contact@union-network.org

Web site: www.union-network.org

Q 15:101.6   How is it possible for an international union to organize U.S. companies?

A good example of how this can happen—offered by President Andy Stern of the Service Employees International Union (SEIU)—was the acquisition of three well-known U.S. security firms by Sweden-based Securitas. The American companies were Pinkerton, Burns International Services, and Loomis Fargo. At about the same time, Group 4 Securicor, a British-Danish outfit, picked up Wackenhut. "All of a sudden," commented Stern, "we found ourselves needing to talk more to CEOs in Europe than in America."

Attorney Gerald Hathaway of the New York firm Littler Mendelson noted that labor organizations are woven into the socio-economic fabric of continental nations such as Germany, where union leaders commonly serve on boards of directors. Unions such as the SEIU are finding that they can deal with these parent corporations, imposing terms and conditions upon their U.S. subsidiaries.

[http://www.workforce.com/archive/feature/24/26/53/index.php?ht=labor%20unions%20labor%20unions]

Q 15:101.7   How do international unions such as UNI seek to bind multinational corporations?

UNI and similar international labor organizations seek to sign so-called "global framework agreements" capable of following the corporation to wherever it establishes operations around the world. The concept of a global agreement is well known in American labor relations, with unions hoping to represent a single employer's employees at multiple locations negotiating for an umbrella agreement that will apply wherever the union later achieves majority support from a location's workforce. [See, e.g., Raley's and United Food and Commercial Workers, 336 NLRB 374 (2001) (The parties attempted to negotiate a global agreement that would cover any future demands for recognition by Local 588. They subsequently signed two separate agreements under which the Respondent recognized Local 588, pursuant to a card check, as the representative of its employees at the Yreka store and at one of the Redding stores.)]

United States Code (U.S.C.)

[References are to question numbers.]

Code of Federal Regulations (C.F.R.)

[References are to question numbers.]

Table of Cases

[References are to question numbers.]

C

D

T

Index

[References are to question numbers.]

Discrimination in employment (*cont'd*)
Title VII. *See* Title VII
wages. *See* Equal Pay Act

Disparate impact
ADEA, 4:148.1
business necessity, 4:38
hiring policies and procedures, 4:38
statistical evidence, 4:38

Disparate treatment
comparative evidence, 4:37
direct evidence, discriminatory motive, 4:37
statistical evidence, 4:37

Docking pay threats and exempt employees, 8:29.1

DOL (Department of Labor). *See specific subject areas of enforcement*

DOT. *See* Department of Transportation

Dress and grooming related to religious beliefs, 4:50

Drug abuse
debarment, 7:216
drug-free awareness program, 7:214
drug policy elements, 7:225
employer policy, 2:42
employer responsibilities, 7:211, 7:213
federal contractors and grant recipients, 7:215–7:220
problem drugs, 7:224
unlawful drug-related activity, 7:212

Drug-Free Workplace Act of 1988, 1:48, 7:120

Drug testing, 3:33, 7:221–7:223
Department of Transportation guidelines, 10:60.1

E

Early retirement
Department of Justice, 10:25
involuntary plans, 4:147
voluntary plans, 4:147.1

Ebola, 15:85

Economic Espionage Act of 1996, 6:46

Educational assistance, 2:25
state universities, in-state tuition for aliens, 12:61.3–12:61.6

EEOC. *See* Equal Employment Opportunity Commission

Electronic Communications Privacy Act of 1986, 5:39

Eleventh Amendment and ADA, 1:45

E-mail, monitoring of, 5:39

Emergency Planning and Community Right to Know Act, 7:126–7:159
chemicals regulated, 7:126–7:132
emergency response plan provisions, 7:147
employer obligations, 7:124, 7:125, 7:134
enforcement by OSHA, 7:156
Hazard Communication Initiative, 7:157–7:159
hazard communication program, 7:122, 7:123
labeling, 7:133
local emergency planning committees, 7:143–7:145
material safety data sheets (MSDS), 7:135–7:137
notification, 7:146, 7:148, 7:149, 7:151, 7:152
"release" defined, 7:149
reporting requirements, 7:153, 7:154
"right-to-know" regulations, 7:121
state emergency response commissions, 7:138, 7:140–7:142
written hazard communication program, 7:132

Emotional distress damages
common law claims, 1:79
FMLA not covering, 1:25, 8:186.2
lie detector tests and, 3:46
Sarbanes-Oxley Act, 9:143

Employee handbooks. *See* Handbooks, employee

Employee Polygraph Protection Act (EPPA), 1:51, 3:44–3:35.2, 6:8
investigation exception under, 3:45.2
national security exemption under, 3:45.1

Employee Retirement Income Security Act (ERISA), 1:7–1:10
abuse of discretion by plan administrator under, 8:112.1
applicability, 8:69, 8:86
binding release of vested pension rights, 8:74
case law, 8:118
civil actions, 8:111
claims by participants, 1:10, 8:112
criminal penalties, 8:110
"defined benefit plan" defined, 8:87, 8:88
"defined contribution benefit plan" defined, 8:89, 8:90

H

M

N

R

T

V

Videotaping and employee surveillance, 5:36

Violations, 8:43. *See also* Penalties
double damages under FLSA, 1:75, 8:48
liquidated damages, 8:44
standing to sue, 8:45
statute of limitations, 8:46
"willful violation" defined, 8:47

Violence in the workplace
action plans, 6:17
ADA interplay, 6:20, 7:233
advice for supervisors, 7:130
Americans with Disabilities Act interplay, 7:233
anthrax or other attack via U.S. Mail, 6:21, 7:234
case law, 7:242
categories, 7:226
collective bargaining relationship, 7:240
common characteristics of perpetrators, 7:227
"criminal endangerment of employees" defined, 6:22
dimensions of workplace violence, 7:236
documenting incidents, 7:229
employee discharge, violence potential, 6:19
evacuation plan, 7:232
federal case law, 7:242
indicia for supervisors to observe, 7:228
labor arbitrator response, 7:241
liabilities to employees and third parties, 6:15
negligent hiring, 6:23, 7:239
OSHA duties, 6:14, 7:235
premises liability, 7:239
preventive measures, 7:231
reducing exposure for violence, 6:16
respondeat superior, 7:239
robbery prevention, 6:25
security experts and consultants, 6:18
third-party perpetrators, 6:24
third-party victims, employer liability to, 7:239
workers' compensation coverage, 7:237, 7:238

Visas
business visitor L-1 visa, 12:128
computer programmers, 12:78
displacement of U.S. employees, 12:69
exchange student visas, 12:124, 12:135
extension of, 12:67
F-1 visas, 12:130, 12:132, 12:133, 12:136
$500 fraud-prevention fee, 12:95
foreign broadcasters, 12:79
H-1B visa, 12:76–12:80, 12:82, 12:89, 12:95, 12:97, 12:134
J-1 visas, 12:135
M-1 visas, 12:137
non-immigration/temporary visas, 12:88, 12:90
$1,000 sponsorship fee, 12:96
student non-immigrant visas, 12:130–12:137
temporary agricultural workers, H2A visa, 12:111–12:113
temporary workers' visa, 12:74, 12:75
TN-1 visas (NAFTA), 12:105–12:110
U.S. Visit program, machine-readable passports, 12:129

Voluntary early retirement plans, 4:147.1

W

W-4 Form, 8:58

Wages. *See* Fair Labor Standards Act (FLSA); Overtime
government contractors. *See* Government contractors

Walsh-Healey Act, 1:6

WARN. *See* Worker Adjustment and Retraining Notification Act

Weingarten rights, 11:39

Whistleblower Protection Act of 1989, 1:59

Whistleblowers, 1:58–1:62. *See also* Government contractors
defined, 1:58
pre-emption, 1:62
punitive damages, 1:60
wrongful discharge claims, 1:61

Wiretapping telephone calls, 5:38

Withholding, 8:54–8:61
legal penalties for improper withholding, 8:60
merit increases versus promotion increases, 8:55
merit-pay procedures, 8:54
part-time employees, 8:56
paycheck deductions, common, 8:57
religious beliefs, 8:59
tax deductions, 8:61
W-4 Form, 8:58